1/04

HOW WE
HAVE
CHANGED

HOW WE HAVE CHANGED

America Since 1950

By Rick Phalen

PELICAN PUBLISHING COMPANY
Gretna 2003

The word "Pelican" and the depiction of a pelican are trademarks
of Pelican Publishing Company, Inc., and are registered
in the U.S. Patent and Trademark Office.

Library of Congress Cataloging-in-Publication Data

How we have changed : America since 1950 / [edited] by Rick Phalen.
   p. cm.
Includes index.
  ISBN 1-58980-110-5 (alk. paper)
  1. United States—Civilization—1945- 2. United States—Social
conditions—1945- 3. National characteristics, American. 4.
Celebrities—United States—Interviews. I. Phalen, Richard C., 1937-
  E169.12 .H677 2003
  973.92—dc21

               2002015406

Printed in the United States of America

Published by Pelican Publishing Company, Inc.
1000 Burmaster Street, Gretna, Louisiana 70053

to Griff

May we know unity . . . without conformity.

Dwight D. Eisenhower

Contents

Metamorphosis

Acceleration

Acknowledgments

I would like to thank everyone who participated in the creation of this book. They represent a broad range of Americans: writers, historians, commentators, entertainers, professionals, and informed citizens. All were generous with their time and I greatly appreciate their interest and cooperation. My colleague and friend Alice Vazquez has assisted me for over eleven years, and her help and advice I hold in the highest esteem.

Introduction

In February 1950, Joe McCarthy announced there were 205 communists in the State Department. He proclaimed that if we cleaned up the State Department and rid ourselves of its communist traitors the Cold War could be won cheaply.

Many bought this specious argument. Serving as a condiment to his crusade, important Russian spies such as Julius and Ethel Rosenberg, David Greenglass, Judith Copeland, and Alger Hiss were apprehended. Although the intellectual community defended them, most others did not, fueling a division that would grow over time, further separating liberals and conservatives.

On June 25, 1950, North Korean troops invaded South Korea, giving the Cold War a new, deadly dimension. It was a United Nations action, but the United States supplied the largest force. Containment and a determination to prevail now marked American foreign policy. Our historic strategy of isolationism became a thing of the past as we established treaties and alliances to circle and contain the communist threat.

During the 1950s, the Cold War firmly established an "us against them" mentality, aided by McCarthy's irresponsible behavior. If it had not been for ABC's need for daytime programming, the Army-McCarthy Hearings would not have been televised and Joe McCarthy's career might not have been effectively ended with his censure in December 1954.

Television was absent when Rosa Parks took that fateful bus ride on December 1, 1955, but made up for it in September 1957 with its coverage of the Little Rock crisis. With *Brown v. Board of Education* in 1954, school segregation was declared unlawful. Television now showed segregation and racism at Little Rock and the nation was appalled. This was a major turning point in the civil rights movement and television would now be its constant companion.

Bill Haley's "Rock Around the Clock" was the number one record in July 1955. It would forever change music, creating new careers while destroying others. From this innocent start until today, it has been blamed for many of society's ills, with layers of generational annoyance to show for all the noise.

President Eisenhower wished to forge peace with Russia but no one knew how to stop the Cold War. Kennedy and the Democrats thought him too conservative; they wished to increase spending, enlarge American arms production, and extend our global commitments. Kennedy said a new generation was coming to power with new ideas *to get the country moving again,* but not specifying where we were going. Ike thought America could no longer shape events; Kennedy disagreed.

JFK failed in his handling of the Cuban invasion in April 1961, redeeming himself while directing the Cuban Missile Crisis the next year. Many believed this to be a major turning point in world history. His presidency ended on November 22, 1963, leaving to speculation how he would have handled the turbulent years that followed, assuming he would have been re-elected.

His successor, Lyndon Johnson, made liberal/conservative more consequential than simply Democrat/Republican, with profound cultural significance as the century progressed. In May 1964 LBJ called for an anti-poverty program, entitling it "The Great Society." By October 1964 Congress had approved eighty-nine Great Society bills. Johnson won the 1964 presidential election, gaining 61 percent of the vote, with the liberals proclaiming that this proved there was no significant conservative movement in America. Many did not notice that Barry Goldwater took five deep southern states–a portent of things to come.

Johnson's Great Society and the Vietnam War lost popularity simultaneously. The Great Society did little for the average white adult, who felt the government was becoming more intrusive and that they were receiving nothing in return. Vietnam was costly in lives and emotion; increasingly people could not understand why we were there and they wanted out.

By 1968 it was evident there was a shift in American culture, with sides forming and alliances shaping. The liberals, intellectuals, and young were against the war, Johnson, and racism. The conservatives considered the counter-culture the dregs of society, culturally subversive and economically parasitic. Not since the Civil War had the country been so divided and polarized.

The Tet Offensive proved we were not winning the war. Martin

Luther King and Bobby Kennedy were assassinated. There were riots in the cities, campuses erupted, and the 1968 Democratic Convention underlined the alienation that pervaded the country. The generation who had fought World War II were estranged from the America of their sons and daughters.

Liberals despised Richard Nixon, but he served them well by conceiving the EPA [Environmental Protection Agency] and OSHA [Occupational Safety and Health Administration]. His secretary of labor fashioned the Philadelphia Plan, America's first racial quota system.

Nixon continued the anti-poverty program, desegregated Southern schools, initiated the first national environmental policies, and opened China—all before Watergate. But Watergate destroyed his presidency. He resigned August 9, 1974, and few people were sad to see him go.

This was sweet revenge for the liberals; for Alger Hiss, McCarthy, for humiliating George McGovern in 1972, Haiphong, Cambodia, Kent State, and gas shortages. A cultural rupture now surrounded us: music was becoming drug oriented, movies more violent, pornography readily available, and younger people questioning authority.

The nation was polarized—even our unceremonious exit from Vietnam in 1973 did not relieve the disruption—liberal/conservative, men versus women, black against white, young versus old, pro-war/anti-war.

By 1980 America had tired of Jimmy Carter, a man determined to convince us our best days were past and who seemed to be trying to make it a self-fulfilling prophecy. Reagan easily beat Carter—51 percent to 41 percent—taking over a country that along with everything else had two oil-related recessions, "tax-bracket creep," and "stagflation."

Reagan cut taxes dramatically, along with the budget. Reagan recognized Russia would never dominate us because they did not have the economic power to do so. He began talking with Gorbachev, at the same time spending large amounts on our military, convincing the Russians they could not compete with us. Reagan admitted involvement in Iran-Contra, but was hazy about events and his popularity suffered. Looking confused and not in control, it was not his finest hour.

With all his talk of government waste, Reagan never submitted a balanced budget, was hurt by Iran-Contra, and at times seemed detached from the presidency. But he was widely admired, helped break the back of communism, and gave America a spiritual rebirth that helped ease the hostility and animosity that had been prevalent in our culture the previous twenty years.

Reagan was a tough act to follow and George Bush could not pull it off. He walked into a recession that ran its course just before he left office. This, coupled with *"Read my lips, no new taxes,"* sank his ship. He was effective directing the Gulf War, but many believe he should have destroyed Saddam Hussein's regime while he had the opportunity, particularly in view of September 11, 2001.

Though communism was in its death throes, Bush made an effort to support Gorbachev, hoping reforms could be installed in the Soviet Empire and stability restored. Bush was concerned that an uncontrollable situation might unfold and was more intent on saving Gorbachev than encouraging the Soviet Republics and satellites to demand their freedom.

This was an interesting political and cultural transition: the country had been fighting communism since 1947; now a moderately conservative president was more intent on working out an accommodation with the communist regime in which he had over invested than in risking possible turmoil by encouraging democratic reforms.

Bill Clinton was arguably the best American politician in the twentieth century. He recognized that culturally the country had changed— he was a product of the '60s—and was convinced the toleration born of the '60s gave him leeway to push the envelope in the '90s.

He fooled few, but this did not matter: nearly 80 percent believed he committed perjury, but more than 60 percent wished him to stay in office. In fact, because the Monica Lewinski affair involved sex, as high as 76 percent believed it should not be pursued.

Many Baby Boomers felt the '60s was a battleground for needed cultural changes, a fight for the personal freedom they enjoy today. They gave Clinton a pass, believing that a large segment of the country deals in moral absolutes, one of many things they fought against in the '60s. They considered his critics zealots, hostile to the zeitgeist of the '60s, believing Clinton should be protected for emotional reasons if nothing else. Many suspect Clinton knew this from the start.

Traditionalists are concerned that Clinton is a portent of things to come. Raised believing in duty, honor, and country, they believe far too many people have only a half-hearted affection for honesty, propriety, and morality. Believing these values have diminished since 1950, they question the future of the nation with our significant drug and crime problem, a population demanding more special assistance, where politically correct masks and distorts reality, popular entertainment debases and ridicules proper behavior, and politicians play to television.

At the conclusion of World War II, Americans were proud of themselves and the country. People were anxious to live the American Dream. We succeeded and became rich beyond our expectations, but the process lowered our standards, eroded personal responsibility, and promoted dependency and victimization.

But the events of September 11, 2001, put things in a different light. America has taken stock of what it has, and what it represents. We had become complacent and self-centered, but again, as so often in the past, we will prove to the world and to ourselves why we are the greatest nation on earth by overcoming our enemies and prevailing.

How We
Have
Changed

PART I

Crossing the Rubicon

Dan Peterson

Peterson was a very successful basketball coach in the United States and Europe. He lives in Milan, Italy, and is Italy's favorite sports commentator. Growing up in the United States, he remembers a man who struck terror in the hearts of many Americans.

A kid down the street named Ralph Chute had just graduated from high school in 1950. He was a great guy. He always chose me in neighborhood softball games, though I was much younger than everyone else. One day word came: "Ralph Chute was killed in Korea." I had an awful time with that for months. Now communism had become my enemy on a first-person basis.

Many guys slightly older than I had joined the Reserves. When the war broke out, those Reserves, most of them 17 and 18, were called up. Some still had a year of high school to go. Another slightly older kid named Jimmy Schutz was called up, as was Jim Marshall, older brother of Jack Marshall, one of my closest friends. So, the Korean War was all around me and had me involved personally.

At the start of 1950, things were abundantly clear: the USSR was our prime enemy. They had the atomic bomb, they had purchased the secrets for the atomic bomb through devious means, they wanted to rule the world, they would use force to do it. Stalin was far worse than Hitler, there was a Cold War, they were saying *nyet!* in the UN, and, worst of all, there were spies in our midst. Who would smoke them out? Up stepped Joe McCarthy.

He set his course on anti-communism in 1950, January 7, 1950, to be precise, at a dinner with some prominent anti-communists. McCarthy was up for re-election in 1952 and one of the dinner guests, Father Edmund A. Walsh, brought up the subject of needing an issue. McCarthy lit up, *That's it! The government is full of communists. We can hammer away at that.*

He was an unusual man for the job, vulnerable to attack on many fronts: special interests, [he] played the lobby game, [was] a gambler and heavy drinker, and a liar, passing off an accident in the Marines in World War II as a battle wound. But he was a born politician, a worker, ambitious, a man who loved to speak in public and who perfected the technique.

He spoke at the Republican Women's Club in Wheeling, West Virginia, on February 9th, 1950, and delivered his famous statement that he had in his hand a list of 205 known communists in the State Department. All hell broke loose, but that didn't slow him down as he repeated the speech across the nation, changing the number of communists each time he spoke.

Sen. Joe McCarthy had found a nerve. Funds came pouring in. It is said he diverted most to his bank account to invest in the stock market or waste on gambling. But he was backed to the hilt. Today it is fashionable to criticize McCarthy, but his poll numbers showed him with well over 50 percent approval ratings. The greatest demagogue in United States political history had the backing of the majority of the people.

There is no calculating the people he ruined. He was close to the truth, but didn't have proof to back it up. Recently declassified documents from the CIA and KGB confirm there were, indeed, communists in the government, exactly as McCarthy had said. The problem was that McCarthy thought he could bluster his way through, that accusations would suffice. They did, for a while.

No group was safe. It was said that blacks were susceptible to the lure of communism, as they were poor and disenfranchised. No less than Jackie Robinson, who broke baseball's color barrier in 1947, came forward to testify in 1949 that his people were not communists.

Hollywood also took a hit. Actors, producers, directors, and others were destroyed when the House Un-American Activities Committee asked if they were communists or not. Those who could not or would not answer, found they were "blacklisted" in Hollywood. Others denied affiliation but were smeared anyway. Some testified against others, as did Oscar-winning director Elia Kazan, a pariah in Hollywood fifty years later. It was ugly.

In April 1954, McCarthy made a big mistake: he took on the U.S. Army. The world would be watching. In fact, the so-called Army-McCarthy Hearings had twenty million television viewers daily, a staggering number in 1954, representing about 50 percent of the households in the country. No one had ever had an audience like this—and we weren't the only ones watching.

President Dwight D. Eisenhower had followed the McCarthy goings-on from the start. In fact, during his 1952 presidential campaign he had stumped for McCarthy in Wisconsin, helping the Senator get re-elected. Ike was criticized for this and it revealed the clout McCarthy had.

Ike now drew the line. He did not openly oppose McCarthy or his methods, but he turned some powerful machinery on him and backed his secretary of the Army, George Stevens, to the hilt. You couldn't go around accusing high-ranking Army officers of being communists under Eisenhower and expect to get away with it. What is more, McCarthy crossed the wrong man in the hearings, Army attorney Joseph N. Welch.

More importantly, McCarthy had earned the enmity of America's foremost television news commentator, Edward R. Murrow. Murrow was a true giant in the industry, a living legend. In 1954 no one challenged Joe McCarthy. To do so was to call attention to yourself and have his wrath turned on you like a white flame. Everyone laid low and hoped he would not see them. He had the mass media cowed, terrified, but not Murrow.

Murrow challenged McCarthy publicly on March 9, 1954 on his television program "See it Now." Murrow said, "Show us your proof." McCarthy had no proof. He was bluffing. He was all form and no substance. Murrow used film footage of McCarthy in action and commented that the man was unscrupulous. A "god" had spoken and McCarthy had been condemned.

On the heels of Murrow came Joseph Welch, the Army's attorney. McCarthy could not compete with the brilliant, impeccable, articulate, and totally honest Welch. It was all over in a matter of days. Welch, after McCarthy attacked one of his people in the hearing, looked at McCarthy and said: "Until this moment, Senator, I think I never really gauged your cruelty or your recklessness. Have you no sense of decency, Sir?"

The effect was devastating and total.

In all of this, even the Senate had been reluctant to raise a hand against McCarthy. Again, it was the times; to be anti-McCarthy branded you as pro-communist. So even the cream of the Senate was reluctant to make a move until Murrow and Welch had taken their respective stands, Murrow exposing McCarthy as a bluff, Welch exposing him as a bully. With this, the Senate censured McCarthy, on a 67-22 vote, on December 2, 1954.

This was only the third such censure in 165 years and stressed the abuses of his senatorial powers and "conduct contrary to senatorial traditions." It was all downhill from there. Already a heavy drinker, McCarthy drank even more. He died on May 2, 1957, of cirrhosis of the liver. He'd gone from being a hero to an outcast in merely seven years. Though he looked much older, he was only 49 at his death.

It's impossible to add up all the damage he inflicted. One thing is clear: no one he accused was ever convicted of being a communist or of having committed a treasonable act on behalf of communism.

In the irony of all ironies, McCarthy's humiliation and fall was a great benefit to the anti-anti-communists. In other words, the pro-communists now had a bulletproof cover. You could no longer call someone a communist or you earned the label "McCarthyite." So, the moles had a free run thanks to the misdirected efforts of Joe McCarthy.

The name Joseph McCarthy carries shame even today. There are people in their 80s who were ruined by him. Earning accolades early on, he later earned epithets. He remains one of the most controversial figures in the history of the U.S. Senate. But he had his own form of genius. He understood the basics that still apply today: scandal, television, Congress. An explosive cocktail.

Whenever I hear someone describe TV or music or journalism or cinema as shocking, I think of where shocking really started. Why the shock approach? To gain attention. If you are 17 on the shock scale today, you must be at least 18 tomorrow or people will tune you out. You must top yourself.

Thus, if Ice-T takes rap music to one level, Eminem must take it to another level. If *Silence of the Lambs* takes film violence to one level, *Natural Born Killer* must top that. If there is a Monica Lewinsky story today, there must be an impeachment tomorrow.

McCarthyism even today is synonymous with "ungrounded accusations." Some revisionists have tried to resuscitate his image after the declassification of those CIA and KGB documents confirmed what McCarthy had been saying . . . but could not prove. Too late, as Joseph McCarthy remains engraved on the American mind as . . . our most hated Senator.

Why did Joseph McCarthy fail in his mission? Theories abound, but the most plausible remains the simplest: he was more interested in grandstanding than in the facts. In baseball terms, he was a "hot dog."

There are other reasons for his demise. Certainly one was challenging the integrity of the U.S. Army. Inferring national hero Gen. George C. Marshall [was] a communist was simply political and public relations suicide.

He died before the Vietnam War, but by now the anti-anti-communists had a free hand. No longer were people reluctant to criticize the U.S. Government for intervention against communism. People protested, dodged the draft, burned flags. Now the anti-communists were reluctant to voice their opinions.

Joe McCarthy set the tone for much that occurred during the last half of the 20th century. He was the Father of Shock, grandstanding on TV in the early 1950s. All future scandals followed his lead over the past fifty years of American culture.

Television, film, and music companies are constantly looking for the next big scandal. McCarthy whetted the U.S. appetite for such things and Richard Nixon, O.J. Simpson, Bill Clinton, and others have simply fueled the fire that he started fifty years ago, a fire that is still raging in all sectors of American life.

America has changed over the last fifty years and for the worse. No one in his right mind would pick up a hitch-hiker today; but no one thought twice about it in 1950. In 1950 no one thought about drugs, school shootings, missing children, sexual abuse, child pornography, and falling test scores. But they are realities today, and that is only a short list of such problems.

Do we blame Joe McCarthy for all that and more? No, that's not possible. The point is this: he set the tone, set the table, and set the pace. In his ignorance, he was a genius. He was like many so-called "artists" of today: it doesn't matter if you are good; what matters is drawing attention. Who cares if that singer cannot sing? He has production, technology, and one hell of a video.

That was Joe McCarthy: all video and no talent. He had what I call SST before there were SSTs: Scandal, Senate, Television. Put them together and you have an audience. Joe McCarthy grasped that. He had scandal with the issue of communists in government, the Senate with his hearings, and the vehicle was television. He hit the mother lode for national fame.

But he failed in his declared mission. He did not convict a single person of being a communist or of committing treasonous or criminal acts in the name of communism, but he gave rise to the anti-anti-communist cause. He remains the man who made being important . . . important.

His was the first major ego fed by TV. All others who followed are his children, his grandchildren or stepchildren. He may not have crushed communism, but he certainly gave rise to the attention-seeking culture in America today. His legacy lives on, stronger than ever.

Richard Fried

A professor of recent American history at the University of Illinois—Chicago since 1972, Fried has written two books on Joe McCarthy. He believes America had already lost the solidarity of World War II when McCarthy made headlines in February 1950, and that he poisoned the political climate far past his time in power.

There is a sense the country was united during World War II but that is a bit deceptive, for there were many divisions. Still, what Americans remembered—and many experienced—was unity. Even before the war was over, some observers began to lament the end of wartime unity. Civic leaders became concerned that postwar conditions were eroding that unity.

At many levels they sensed a pervasive selfishness, and feared Americans were identifying not as citizens of a totality, but as members of smaller, more parochial groups—labor unions being an obvious instance. Much of the politics of the late '40s, and after, was about trying to bring things back together.

The effort was not particularly successful, and various critics of the centrifugal tendencies in American society nominated different groups as the culprits. "Communist influences" were one obvious candidate for blame, and that's where Joseph R. McCarthy came in.

"McCarthyism" is a convenient name that people on both sides applied and continue to apply to a deep running phenomenon. It's easy to talk about McCarthyism; it's a nice, neat label, but it's a label for a very sloppy and diffused set of social and political phenomena, something much broader than the antics and exertions of the senator himself.

The institutional aspects of what we came to call McCarthyism— loyalty oaths, loyalty and security programs, broadcast accusations of disloyalty—mostly predated McCarthy himself. To his advantage, he managed to identify himself closely with these developments and with the communist issue and thus to take historical credit for things most of which he did not invent.

At the time there were questions and doubts about national identity, and McCarthy was able to play on these. But these were eventually going to be resolved with or without McCarthy. Take the rise of mass consumption, for example: in the 1950s we experienced a prosperity that in a way made McCarthyism over the long term impossible. William Levitt made the remark that a guy who owns his own home is going to be so busy he doesn't have time to be a communist. He also, I would add, is not going to have time to be much of a McCarthyite.

McCarthy voted fairly conventionally as a Republican, but he certainly had no great reputation as a budget cutter. In fact, in early 1950 he was briefly enthusiastic about a super Social Security program to enlarge retirement benefits. His critics said it was like Dr. [Francis] Townsend's program in the 1930s and, like that scheme, fiscally irresponsible. He dropped the idea at the point he was beginning to focus exclusively on the communist issue.

Using McCarthy's name as a label for a broader set of phenomena, which for rough convenience we might call "excess anti-communism," was handy, but entailed disadvantages. His ability to identify with this issue, and his opponents' complicity in that identification, had the tendency to inflate people's perception of how powerful he was.

The communist issue was a factor, though not often a major one, in the 1950 [elections] and, to an even lesser extent, the 1952 elections, but McCarthy, by managing to achieve a unique identification with that issue, managed to foster the sense that he was a critical factor in the results. He was not a real factor in 1952 at all, though he was a very visible presence.

When he became a discredited figure in 1954, this had the effect of discrediting the more hard-nosed version of anti-communism he professed. Some perceptive conservatives at the time, notably Whittaker Chambers, saw and lamented this effect. Conservatives in the 1980s would also come to rue the extent to which the term "McCarthyism" could be used as a club by the Left. When we got rid of McCarthy, we got rid of extreme anti-communism, which is good from my point of view, but we also got a heavy but imprecise rhetorical club which some groups on the left were able to use rather too facilely.

In the late 1950s and beyond, to the resurgent right, many things had gone wrong, some political, but many moral. Conservatives in the broadest, least sectarian sense of the term might rue the decline of a simpler, small-town-oriented life rich in face-to-face personal relationships. The evaporation of this older sort of community and the coming of the larger society were accompanied by the rise of remote systems of power and the loss of individual control.

Some people saw in McCarthy a lever to use against such loss of control. Some Americans tried to reassert control through religion. Some of them—as well as conservatives of a more secular bent—got the notion to mobilize politically. The Goldwater movement became a vehicle for them, a vehicle beyond the intentions of Goldwater himself.

I don't see Goldwater as a conscious leader of such a social movement. His candidacy did mobilize and did benefit from an effort by conservatives to control the Republican Party in the '60s. That was the real trend going on, and what looked like a colossal disaster for them in the wake of Goldwater's 1964 defeat was actually a victory in that the GOP would come under increasingly conservative direction from that point forward.

In the late '60s, there was a sense of disorder in American life. Vietnam was distant, but what were not distant were the anti-Vietnam protests in the streets, and these became associated in the public mind with other forms of disorder. The smarter student protestors very quickly understood that they had acquired a negative power—whatever they were protesting against had a tendency to swing significant groups the other way. Thus, while on balance the '60s moved us culturally to the left, politically it was the right which would benefit.

During the 1950s, much of what happened culturally was largely independent of politics. It was prosperity, demography, the baby boom, and attitudes promoted by economic plenty. Sometimes politics was not so much what was moving the vehicle as the vehicle that was being moved by deeper social changes.

Elmer Bernstein

One of Hollywood's greatest composers, Bernstein won an
Academy Award for *Thoroughly Modern Millie.* He has written the
music for a host of other films such as *The Magnificent Seven, The
Man With the Golden Arm, My Left Foot,* and *The Ten Commandments.*
He was investigated by the House Un-American Activities
Committee in 1955 regarding a possible communist affiliation,
which resulted in his being "graylisted"—working, but not making much money. It took the intervention of Cecil B. DeMille to
have him "unlisted."

I came to Hollywood in August 1950. At the time, the major studio
apparatus was still in place. Harry Cohn was the head of Columbia,
Jack Warner was the head of Warner Brothers, Louis B. Mayer was at
MGM, [Darryl] Zanuck was at Fox, and they still had contract players.

In fact, after I did my first film for Sidney Buchman, who was then
vice president of Columbia Pictures, the first thing Harry Cohn did
was to offer me a seven-year contract; they still had those kinds of
things. I very wisely turned it down. Wisely, because they were sort of
chattel contracts, and independence was already in the air by 1950.

The studios were in some ways very comfortable places. They were
quite grand. They had wonderful cottages for the stars. Wonderful
offices for the people who worked there. They had tremendous back-
up because they were heavily staffed. If you were a composer, you had
an office and a librarian to help you with anything you needed. It was
in many ways a very comfortable situation.

I remember the first time I ever saw Harry Cohn. I was having a
meeting with my producer, Sidney Buchman, who, as I say, was his
vice president. I was coming up to the office and this rather large
man was backing out of the office. I remember he had a huge red
flower in his buttonhole and a jacket that looked like a horse blanket. He was backing out, absolutely purple with rage, and screaming
at the top of his lungs, "You're a thousand percent wrong!"

That's the first time I'd heard that kind of mathematics. I walked in and said, "Sidney, I presume that was Harry Cohn."

He said, "Absolutely!"

I never met Louis B. Mayer, unfortunately. I did meet Jack Warner because I did a picture over there. He was a very, very colorful character. Harry Cohn wanted to entertain the public. Warner went a step further. He wanted to entertain the public, but he had the sense that he had some intellectual responsibility.

He did, in fact, develop a studio full of pretty good writers. He did some fairly serious subjects. He was a very colorful character who couldn't say a single sentence without a few four-letter words. A writer friend of mind told me this story about Warner:

> He had a party at his house. It was a weekend, daytime, and he had his infant son with him who fell into the pool and he jumped in and saved him. Later he ran into Jack Warner, and he said, "We had the most terrible time back there in the pool. The kid almost drowned." And Warner said to him, "Well, don't worry about it. We're insured."

One of the things that hurt the studios was that the pioneer guys like Sam Goldwyn, Harry Cohn, and Jack Warner were getting old. They'd had their great pioneering days and, quite honestly, I don't think they kept up with what was happening with the advent of television. Instead of realizing what an amazing tool television was going to be, they fought it all the way.

In fighting television, they found that they had these vast studios with tremendous overhead. The number of pictures they had been making diminished because people began to watch television. They weren't going to the movies that much anymore. I think it was lack of forward vision. They'd run out of vision.

I was caught up in the "blacklisting" of the '50s. I think one of the things that happened to everybody, on every level, was fear. It was a fascinating phenomenon, looking back at it now. I remember experiencing the fear. It is amazing what fear these people were able to generate. I mean, '53-'54-'55—we were less than ten years away from Hitler.

It seems funny now, imagining a communist threat in the United States. It's a joke. We had to worry about the Soviet Union, that's different. But internally, it was a joke. Most of these guys were clowns. What they did do successfully was to instill fear, and that's what you remember most from that period—fear. If somebody was named a Red, did you want to associate with them? Did you want to be seen in public with him? They did a very, very good job of that, and it really worked. But the reason it worked was that they were able to frighten the studio heads.

It started at the top. There used to be a morals clause in every contract in those days. In the '20s, with the Fatty Arbuckle—Virginia Rapp scandal, movies began to get a reputation for being immoral and full of immoral people. They were very worried about public relations. They got this czar, Will Hayes, to make sure everything was sanitized. So the heads were very vulnerable to feelings of where the public was, so to speak. And they were afraid that these Un-American Activities people would convince them (the public) that Hollywood had a communist hue.

My official status in those days—because there were fine gradations—I would have been "graylisted" rather than "blacklisted." "Graylisted" was when they weren't sure you were a card-carrying member of the Communist Party, which I wasn't. But if they weren't sure, they wouldn't put you on a list where you couldn't work at all. I didn't realize I was being listed at all. But I suddenly realized I wasn't working. Finally, I was doing things like *Robot Monster*. I got $800 to compose, orchestrate, and conduct. That was $800 for two months' work.

I believe somebody in the Allied Artists' organization let it slip that I was in trouble. There was a guy called Mike Connelly. He was [with] the *Hollywood Reporter*. He carried an item in his column that I had been named, among others. He said, "So far, none of these people has come forward to either confirm or deny."

When this happened, I was working for Cecil B. DeMille. He had engaged me to work on *The Ten Commandments*. DeMille called me into his office when it became public. I was very fond of him. I know he is a very controversial character, but he was kind and nice to me. Semi-arguably, [he was] the most interesting person I ever worked for.

Anyway, he called me into his office and asked if I was a member of the Communist Party, had I ever been a member of the Communist Party. I did not stand on my constitutional rights to refuse to answer. I said no.

He was very well connected and took it upon himself not to clear me, because he couldn't do that. No person could clear you, so to speak. He spoke to people in Washington—I overheard the phone call—and said he had spoken with me and he was satisfied that I was not a communist. Subsequently, I was called before the House Un-American Sub-committee, but I daresay that without DeMille's intervention in this matter, things probably would have been much more difficult for me.

I was lucky. By the time I was called, McCarthy had been censured and they were being much more careful. This was 1955, and they kept asking me whether anybody I knew was a communist. I replied the only way I could know if anybody was a communist was if they told me they were a communist. That was already inadmissible. They wouldn't allow evidence like that because that was third-person testimony. And obviously, if I weren't at a Communist Party meeting, I couldn't identify anybody as a communist.

I was lucky. Also, DeMille's help had a lot to do with it.

Many people were injured. They were injured in their souls. I believe there were a couple of suicides; illness, people whose lives were never the same, who never recovered their composure or their sense of well-being. There was broad injury.

Robert Ferrell

According to Ferrell, noted presidential historian, 1950 marked the beginning of societal and cultural change in America. President Truman, speaking at the University of Missouri in mid-June 1950, said America was entering a new era of economic prosperity. A few days later, the Korean War broke out and America began a forty-year period of impermanence.

He believes the Korean War was the foundation for the anti-war movement and the riots and protests of the '60s and '70s and that unresolved issues beginning in 1950 have led to a culture much different from that of mid-twentieth century America.

The year 1950 was a turning point in the history of the American people. One employs the phrase with hesitation, as historians, political scientists, and journalists have overused it so often in seeking to make or underline their points. And yet it deserves use, for after the Korean War opened there could be no continuation of the ways of thought that had gone before.

The war introduced a basic uncertainty that marked a new way of thought in the United States and has persisted through the decades that followed, down to the present day. Before that year, 1950, there had been plenty of uncertainty, not least during World War II's opening months when in Asia the forces of Japan seemed capable of carrying everything before them. And in Europe the divisions of Hitler's Germany appeared unconquerable, despite what seemed a setback before the Russian capital. Surely, it seemed, the German armies would take Moscow that difficult (for American and other hard-pressed supporters of freedom) spring of 1942.

But then the World War turned in favor of the democracies and victory finally came. In the next few years uncertainties arose over the behavior of our former Russian ally, causing substantial changes in American-Soviet relations. But even the Cold War, as it was announced by the journalist Walter Lippmann, who took the phrase from a publicist of Bernard Baruch, did not shake the optimism of Americans in the way that the Korean War did.

Despite the invocation of such anti-Russian measures as the Truman Doctrine, the Marshall Plan, and the North Atlantic Treaty Organization, the people of the United States retained their feeling for a continuing improvement in international relations and in their domestic concerns, until the coming of the war in Korea brought their hopes up short, which is the state in which they have been ever since.

The war that opened in 1950 came without warning, and not least to the president of the United States, who early in June of that year traveled to Baltimore to dedicate the new Friendship Airport. He thence flew to Missouri, where he spoke at the University of Missouri in Columbia and then in St. Louis and sounded the most optimistic of notes about the future.

The president told the students in Columbia, and repeated the message to his audience in St. Louis, that the American nation was about to enter a new era of indefinite prosperity. He reasoned that World War II, despite the consequent troubles with Russia, had ensured the end of wars large and small, that the nations had tired of conflict and understood at long last their futility, and that everything had opened for a lasting development of economies everywhere that would ensure the development of the human spirit.

In his enthusiasm for the wonderful prospect he was holding before his auditors, the president was reminded when speaking to the two thousand friendly students who stood before him at the university in Columbia of the lines from Tennyson's "Locksley Hall" that he had written out years before when he was in high school and had carried ever since in his billfold—lines he had rewritten again and again as he contemplated them, the pages frayed from use over the years.

He spoke earnestly to the students about the new reality predicted by the poet long before—Tennyson had seen the future when he wrote at the height of the Victorian Age—about a time when the battle flags would be furled in the Parliament of Man.

The Korean War rudely interrupted the presidential prediction and changed the confidence that had preceded it.

One of the changes was a feeling, sure and confirmed, that America was being attacked by foreigners and fellow travelers within its midst. They had observed the two trials of the former state department employee, a graduate of the Harvard Law School, Alger Hiss, who in 1950 was convicted and sent to prison actually for refusing to admit that he had known his accuser.

But to the American public the issue had been one of Hiss's spying for Soviet Russia. Meanwhile, President Truman had confirmed his concern over spies and spying by creating a federal loyalty program that involved questioning all federal employees to discern if they had been disloyal.

The Korean War then gave an opportunity for a hitherto obscure Wisconsin senator, Joseph R. McCarthy, who for several years would hold national attention as he asserted the intrusion of agents and spies into the very heart of American government.

The marked sense of unease—some described it as a national malaise that came with the Korean War—was caused in some part by the war's uncertain origin—uncertain until the opening of Soviet archives many years later showed that the North Koreans, who desired to take over South Korea, had received the green light from the Soviets.

The Russian government then controlled by Joseph Stalin had not merely trained the North Korean army and given it planes and tanks that the South Koreans had been refused by the United States, but had encouraged it to attack. At the time this was not too clear, although the Truman administration believed it to be the case.

Korea supported the feeling of the American people that the war possessed an undefinable danger and in itself was almost incomprehensible. The intervention of the government of mainland China confirmed this feeling. There followed the near rolling up of the American Eighth Army in the war's initial months, when the attempt by Gen. Douglas MacArthur to occupy all of Korea brought the Chinese intervention and the driving of American forces south of the 38th parallel, the border between the two Koreas.

From that point, the Americans under Gen. Matthew B. Ridgeway rolled back the Chinese and North Koreans to a line roughly that of the 38th parallel. There followed a period of months when the two forces fought a seemingly aimless series of battles for hills and useless territory that did not have much to do with a viable border between the Koreas.

The jousting, for such it seemed, ended not in clear-cut victory for either side (although the United States really had won the war by preventing the overrunning of South Korea and had forced numerous

casualties upon the bunched-up Chinese attackers in November-
January 1950-51), but in a cease-fire that continues to the present
day.

The uncertainties that accompanied the war, including exploita-
tion by the anti-communists such as Senator McCarthy, thereafter
were followed by the Vietnam War in the 1960s and early 1970s and
by other occasions of fighting or threats of fighting that kept before
all Americans the endangered nature of world peace. Vietnam was
not nearly as important as Korea, but it held the world stage for
longer. Together with the collapse of the presidential administration
of Richard M. Nixon in 1974, after months of congressional investi-
gation and preparation for impeachment, Vietnam and Nixon—
almost in the public mind twin disasters—poisoned the wells of public thought in the years after Korea.

Korea, the McCarthy controversy, Vietnam, Nixon, all brought a
belief that the government was something apart from the best in
American life and that the American people had created a monster,
not an instrument for their protection. The sense that government
was the problem flourished in the years after Korea—a silly notion,
but the feeling was undeniable.

Lastly, there were other conclusions drawn or drawable about
Korea, but this one is worth mentioning: the Korean war had much
to do with inspiring changes in American life, American family life.

The Norman Rockwell portraits of family life that flourished in the
Saturday Evening Post in the 1930s and 1940s, however apart from the
reality of divorces and domestic contentions that were present all
along, became explicit in family life after Korea, and some of them
were hardly admirable. The reasons therefore are not easy to state
and may be incapable of definition.

The movement of the American economy to ever higher plateaus
began with the Korean War and had much to do with domestic famil-
ial confusions. With economic plenty, the doubling and tripling of
the American economy that began in 1950, it was possible to do
things that before would have meant personal economic disaster.
Whatever the economy of plenty, some force or forces were at work.

Surely involved was the national unrest that began with Korea.
When two jobs within a single family became possible, notably in the
1970s and thereafter, children within the busy family work ethic
sometimes received less attention than hitherto, and the former

niceties of family life, wherein children behaved themselves generally, and in particular showed care in dealing with their elders, in or out of a family, came to a crashing end.

The Age of Uncertainty began in 1950. Utterly confirming it are the events of September 11, 2001. No one, in or out of New York City, is likely to forget September 11, for the rest of his or her life.

Dick Clark

When ABC went national with "American Bandstand" in 1957, the program became an overnight success. Dick Clark, the host, instantly became the most powerful man in Rock 'n' Roll.

When *"Bandstand"* went on nationally in August 1957, every kid in the world watched it, and radio stations began to copy what was played on television. There were no restrictions on that show. White radio—you couldn't get a black record on the air, that's why there were so many covers (whites singing black hits).

But "Bandstand" was one of the first to play black music. Freed (Allen Freed) aired black artists on his radio station in New York, and when he was in Cleveland, but "Bandstand" was the first national exposure.

Locally, in Philadelphia, when the show was on, there was never any problem playing black-oriented music. That's why it was so popular.

In the mid-'50s I was in my 20s, playing records for a livelihood. My problem was I couldn't convince management to allow me to play "kid music." They insisted we play the old music, then couldn't understand why the audience wasn't young. They called the radio show "The Bandstand," hoping to draw off some of the popularity of the television show. There was a radio show and a television show with the same name running simultaneously—but the radio show was Perry Como, Eddie Fisher, Don Cornell, Ralph Flannigan, and so forth. It was a frustration.

Eventually, bright people in radio began to play *kid music,* and it was highly black-oriented, and that's when they [achieved big ratings].

There was a disc jockey in every town who discovered if you played Rhythm 'n' Blues, or Rockabilly, or anything of that nature, kids would come to you in great numbers.

I remember the period vividly. I was young, impressionable, and very naive, and it was the beginning of everything. I have fond memories of it. The biggest problem you have as you get older is not to hang on to the old days. Let them go, have them become part of your

41

life's scrapbook. I don't think those were the best days of my life, but they made the biggest impression on me because I couldn't ever, in my wildest dreams, believe where my life was going to go.

I'm afraid we won't see those days again. The audience has become far too sophisticated in its tastes. We've raised generations of people who are very particular about what they want to listen to. You see it exemplified in radio formats that proliferate yearly. They're going after narrower and narrower slices of the audience.

It's really hard to visualize the day when Fats Domino, Pat Boone, Perry Como, a big band record, The Chords, The Hilltoppers, Chuck Berry, and Don Cornell were all in the same stack of records.

Arlene Sullivan

The program went on the air at 3 P.M. Eastern Time. Millions of teens would rush home from school to see a studio full of high school kids dance to the latest hits and rate records, and hosted by someone adept at leading this mass of pimples, greasy hair, angst, and teenage affectations. That someone was Dick Clark, the program "American Bandstand," and it was the first teenage dance show televised coast to coast.

Clark, always the master of the situation, created romance and drama for young America in the persons of Arlene Sullivan and Kenny Rossi and Justine Carrelli and Bob Clayton. They were the focal point, the love interests of "Bandstand." The girls thrived on it while the boys put it down. Arlene Sullivan was on "Bandstand" from 1956 to 1960, more than her allotted fifteen minutes.

She was strolling and bopping when Rock 'n' Roll was in its infancy, while television was still experimenting, the performers new and exciting. The sky was bluer, the grass was greener, and the summers were softer. Arlene still gives it a ten, likes the beat, and would certainly buy it—except the studio is empty and the artists are gone.

I first went to "Bandstand" with a couple of friends and it was difficult to get in. If you were a regular, you got in automatically. If you weren't, you'd have to stand in line. They only allowed a certain number of kids in and if you didn't make it, tough luck. We didn't get in that day so we went down to the corner drugstore called Pop Singer's. We were drinking cokes and the next thing you know a lot of the regulars came in from the show and we started to talk.

On our way home we met one of the regulars whose name was Roe and told her we didn't get in that day. She told us to come back and she'd try to get us in. She did and introduced me to a lot of the regulars and they had a party the next week. I went to the party, got to know everyone, and became a regular. By knowing them, I got in—it was who you know. That was the end of '56.

One summer day in 1957 we arrived and there were these huge cameras; completely different cameras than before. They told us we were going national, and you didn't realize what that meant until you started getting letters. When it was a local show, we would get some fan mail, but now I really started getting mail. Dick Clark would interview you on the show, mention your name, ask how old you were and what school you went to. That's how people got to know you.

When it went nationwide, it became a phenomenon; we would get 500 to 1,000 letters a day sometimes. Bob and Justine were the blond couple and Kenny and I were the dark-haired couple. They were very, very popular, probably the most popular couple on the show.

I became a regular before Kenny and was receiving some fan mail and getting noticed a little bit. One day I was on the floor and looked up and saw this cute little guy sitting in the stands and asked him to dance. That was not done in those days, but I asked him to dance because he reminded me of myself.

We liked each other and then he came back and I would get him in and he became a regular. We started dancing together all the time, then kind of became boyfriend and girlfriend. The next thing you know we were a couple and started to get very popular like Bob and Justine.

There was a scandal before Dick Clark took the show over. The DJ before Dick Clark was an alcoholic and got involved with some other people, not kids from the show, but with real young girls. They were caught drinking on somebody's boat or something, a big scandal, and they fired him. They hired Dick Clark and he was squeaky clean and he didn't want to mess up anything. He kept his distance from us so there wouldn't be any scandal. He was nice to us, but he never wanted to get too close.

Dick Clark would go to the suburbs on the weekends and appear at big school dances. We would meet at Pop Singer's and Pop would take us to Dick Clark's dances. Dick really wanted us there. We were a draw.

There were only certain kinds of dances we could do. Dick Clark would not allow us to do a slow dance with a grind in it or anything like that. Any kind of dirty dancing was out. The Stroll came along because this kid Frankie always wanted to make up dances. So he started The Stroll and we all started doing it. The Stroll was a big deal.

We were famous all around the country and when talent that performed on "Bandstand" went to different cities, the kids used to ask them about us. They used to come back and say, "Do you know how popular you are?" We didn't have a clue.

Annette Funicello came on the show and sought me out and said, "Every place I go people say I look like you."

I said, "That's funny, because I get letters saying that you and I resemble one another."

Dick Clark told us that when we became 18 we had to leave the show. Most of us were 17½ or 18, so this was the end. He cut the room in half with the regulars that were so famous. We were gone. Gone. Completely gone. It was like being in the middle of Manhattan one day and then being in the middle of Siberia the next.

We were just totally blown away. He told us the reason he had to get rid of us was because the business people were asking questions about the kids doing commercials. He said because we were not professionals there was no way we could do commercials and because we were amateurs you couldn't be a professional dancer. You couldn't be a professional of any kind.

To dance on the show you had to be an amateur. If you were in a magazine, you were kicked off the show. Once you made a record, you were kicked off the show. Kenny made a record and Dick Clark called him in the office and said that was his last day. One girl was hired by *Teen Magazine* and it made every single newspaper in the United States that she was kicked off.

We were used. It was unbelievable the money that was made from us. The problem is you didn't know. Nobody was greedy.

Sixteen Magazine used me. They would write stories and use my name and give me a few dollars, pay for my New York trips. Then I got a job and got over it. I never took myself seriously, thank God. I never wanted to be a movie star or a singer, but I guarantee if I could sing I probably would have tried it just like some of them did.

The '50s were so great. There weren't any wars, any drugs. Kids did not do a lot of drinking. Smoking was rare, but we all tried it. I think the majority of the kids in the '50s would get in the back seat of a car and they would make out and touch, but nobody really had sex. I didn't have sex when I was a teenager, didn't even think about it. None of my friends did.

The sad part about kids today that are having babies at 12 and 13 years old is they're missing all the fun. The fun part, the exciting part of being a teenager in the '50s, was making out in the back seat and not doing it. Kenny and I did not have sex, we respected one another. He respected me, I respected him. Today we are friends and we still respect one another. We still kid about not doing it and all that stuff.

Kids today don't get it. They really don't get it. It's so sad to see 13-year-old girls having babies and the boys not caring about these little human lives.

It's a lot of things. It's the media. It's the parents. It's the parent not being home when these kids come home from school. It's not having dinner at 5 or 6 o'clock like we used to and everyone [was] at the table. It's not sharing the living room with one TV and everybody watching the same program with your mother and your father and your brother and your sister.

It's having one telephone so when one person's on the phone, you can't be in another room having secrets with anybody else. It's having one automobile and you had to walk. We survived with one car, one telephone, and one TV. Today everybody has to have their own TV, their own phone, their own car, their own computer. Kids have been spoiled, spoiled rotten.

Parents thought kids should have everything they didn't have. I don't agree with that. I didn't have any children, but I probably would have done the same thing. Every Christmas I wanted a bicycle. I never got a bicycle. I won a car on "Bandstand" at 15, and my parents sold the car. I gave them the money and told them to buy a bike for my baby sister. So you see, I didn't have any children and I'm already spoiling my little sister.

It's just unbelievable what they allow now. I know there's freedom of speech but limit [the violence] on TV for kids. I don't like censoring anything. I don't believe in it. I think everybody should do what they want to do. But it's completely out of control, just out of control. It cannot get any worse unless somebody on a music video actually kills somebody. I mean, what else is left?

Shelley C. Rountree

In 1959 people married at an early age, in Shelly's case at 19. Her marriage quickly began to deteriorate, and, not working, she watched a great deal of television, "American Bandstand" being one of her preferred programs. Her favorite couple was Arlene Sullivan and Kenny Rossi, and she would fantasize that her marriage could be as happy as they appeared to be.

Everyone knew Dick Clark and the music he played, but I didn't pay much attention to his program until I moved to Dallas, Texas, with my first husband in 1960. The marriage wasn't going well so I began watching daytime TV to escape the unhappiness of a bad situation. "American Bandstand" was uplifting and romantic and I could identify with it because the people on the program weren't that much younger than I was.

I loved the music and loved to watch the couples dancing and interacting. I, like everyone, liked Dick Clark. I adored watching these happy people and I thought I'd love to feel that way again. They were interesting and I was fascinated by the life they were leading, which was beyond me by that point.

I liked one couple in particular. She was short, and dark, 5-foot-2 at most, and he was taller than she. They looked Italian and just so in love and adorable and were wonderful dancers. I was mesmerized, I couldn't take my eyes off of them.

Once in a while I'd see one of them dance with someone else and it upset me, unhappy to see them not together. Dick Clark mentioned them one time, and I remember the girl's name was Arlene. It's been a long time, but I would know them if I saw them today.

In our day we were innocent, naive, and I'm glad of it. It was the best of times. You grow up too soon as it is and I don't envy those who are growing up today. Now, nothing is sacred.

Kids today are jaded and unhappy because they don't know what morals are. They don't know what it is to wait to experience things as we did.

The music today, if you call it music, is noise and racket. It's sexual, but not romantic. There's no illusion.

The media has exploited people terribly, we've lost our innocence as a nation. We don't need to be naive and stupid, but rather innocent with something to look forward to, to wait for. The romantic aspects are gone. It's sad.

Pat Boone

The year 1957 was a turning point in American culture. Pat Boone, clean-cut, handsome, and attending Columbia University, was an enormous success as a singer. The only singer more popular was Elvis. The majority of America's youth entered Elvis' camp, opting for long hair, surly looks, and muddy lyrics. Not only America, but the world took a turn toward rebelliousness, and things have never been the same since.

Nineteen fifty-seven was a fabulous year for me. I had "Love Letters in the Sand," "April Love," and two movies, *Bernadine* and *April Love*. I was voted the most popular male singer, beating Elvis, but that was the last time.

Elvis was definitely a watershed performer. A white singer who could sound black, though he certainly didn't sound as black as Little Richard or some of the other performers. He opened the door to the acceptance of Rhythm and Blues and I did too in my way because I had the more cleaned-up versions.

My very first record, "Two Hearts, Two Kisses," had me competing with Frank Sinatra, Doris Day. I was unknown, so Randy Wood at Dot Records sent me all over the country to promote it, and I wound up having a hit. So here I was, right out of the chute, competing with Frank Sinatra and Doris Day, not Elvis. Elvis had not had his first record on RCA released yet. Thank goodness for me.

While running around the country there were several times when the promotion guy would bring me into a radio station and say, "I've got young Pat Boone here. He has that record 'Two Hearts, Two Kisses', and the program director would look up at me skeptically and say, 'Sure, that's Pat Boone.'"

He thought Pat Boone was black, so I had captured enough of the flavor, even on "Tutti-Frutti" and "Ain't That A Shame." I had ten or eleven records on the Rhythm and Blues charts and was accepted as a Rhythm and Blues artist, which was very rare for a white guy during that period of the late '50s.

But Elvis, even more of course, sounded like he was influenced by black music. He was knocking the door down because up until then so-called black or race music couldn't be played on most radio stations. Even the phrase Rock 'n' Roll, a euphemism for sex, became accepted.

More and more taboo subjects began to be accepted, experimented with. Elvis in his show was hyper, to say the least, and on "The Ed Sullivan Show" they kept the camera focused above his waist in case his pelvis got to twitching. He became the emblem, the symbol of broken taboos. He was the guy . . . he was the rebel, breaking the restrictions in the code and getting away with it, becoming bigger every day because he was defying accepted cultural tradition, was handsome and charismatic, and the kids loved him and it seemed like nothing could restrain him.

There was a press conference at the time and they asked, "Elvis, when are you going to get married and have kids like Pat Boone?"

He gave that lopsided grin and said, "Why should I buy a cow when I can get milk through the fence?" That sent shock waves through parents, teachers, ministers, and a few legislators around the country.

Elvis was more of an influence, more of a cultural phenomenon, than he knew. I'm giving him the benefit of the doubt, but I don't think he understood the repercussions of some of the things he said. I think he was trying to get a laugh from his buddies. I don't believe Elvis had any notion of the lasting consequences or the influence he was exerting on young people and on the culture. I saw some of it then, and of course I was extremely influence-conscious. I realized from the beginning that if I had influence, and if kids were going to imitate me in any way, I wanted it to be a positive influence.

I wrote a book, *Twixt 12 and 20,* which was a non-fiction bestseller for two years, and I said, "Whether we want to be role models or influences or not, we are, because kids tend to imitate people they admire and look up to." I wanted to be a good influence.

I was lampooned for that. People sneered at the idea that an entertainer had to try to be a good influence on his fans. Sinatra at the time was asked about being a good influence and said, "I owe my public nothing but a good performance. What I do in my own private life is my business."

Well, it's his business alright, but it's reported universally so it is an influence on others. I've always felt we owe our fans the best we have to offer, including our behavior, which they're going to emulate.

The Rolling Stones, and so many of the acts of the '60s, sang about and bragged about their drug usage, the groupies and the sex, and kids thought that was great. So they, in their own spheres, would try to emulate and get away with the same things. So many singers after Elvis brought bottles of Jack Daniels on stage—Jim Morrison was one—and would wave the bottle and say, "This is my inspiration." The kids would say, "Right on," and they started smoking pot and using other drugs. It was a progression.

I don't think you can blame pot, alcoholism, and drug usage on Elvis. What he did was unintentional. Elvis opened the door to this rebellious attitude that kids could reject the moral teachings of their parents and their predecessors and do their own thing. Jerry Rubin said *if it feels good—do it*. Elvis was the precursor, the trailblazer of this attitude.

I told him once, "Elvis, I felt sorry for you when I saw you on TV that first time."

He said, "Sorry for me? Why?"

I said, "Well, that hip problem. I know it was embarrassing."

He said, "Oh, man, I can't help it."

I said, "What do you mean, you can't help it?"

He said, "Well I don't know. The music starts and something comes over me. I just can't help it."

I said, "If you can't help it, I am in trouble because I *can* help it."

How was I going to compete with that?

The kids thought it was terrific, that's what they wanted to do. They felt urges, too. They wanted to let them go and here was their idol encouraging and exemplifying it, dating one starlet after another and saying openly, *I don't need to settle down and get married 'cause I can get my milk through the fence.*

He and I visited each other in our homes in Bel Air. We lived for many months just a few blocks apart. I would visit him sometimes in the evening and he had a couple from Memphis that would cook for him, take care of his house. His dates consisted of having one of his buddies go pick up a starlet or a young girl, bring her to his house, and Elvis would go over and kiss her and introduce her around.

They'd laugh and kiss and maybe have something to drink and

we'd have chicken-fried steak, okra, black-eyed peas, cornbread and that food from Memphis. Then he'd say, "You all excuse me. I want to show (the girl's name) something," and he would disappear to another part of the house. The stag party would carry on and then after a while she'd come back with him and he'd have one of his buddies take her home. That was her date with Elvis.

He'd come to my house and the contrast was incredible. He'd come up with a buddy or two and have his collar turned up, his dark glasses, his jumpsuit, and get out of his Rolls and walk around to the back where he heard us splashing in the pool with our four daughters. They didn't know much about him except he was a friend. They liked him. They knew he liked them. So they would run across the grass and jump up on him. They'd be sopping wet and get him wet, and I'd say, "Girls, girls, hey, wait a minute."

Elvis would say, "Leave 'em alone. I love it."

And he did.

He wanted so much to have a wife and kids and family. He knew he was missing all that. I didn't know at the time that he had Priscilla stashed at Graceland. Of course they got married and had one child but he never relinquished his buddies.

He'd be in Palm Springs. There'd be two or three of his buddies in his house all the time and now his wife was the one he took into another part of the house. They tried to have a life, but his buddies were always welcome. Priscilla had gotten used to that back at Graceland, but nothing much changed after they got married. His existence was always a strange, cluttered one, and not the life he really wanted. But he just didn't feel secure without his buddies around.

Now it's a new era. There is a stirring of the old American spirit. Once we were attacked and confronted, as horrifically as we were, you have seen the flags break out. Wal-Mart, Target, all the stores— they just can't supply the flags fast enough.

There has been a generation of kids not learning, not being exposed to patriotic songs. "I'm Proud To Be An American" and "This Is My Country" were never heard. The parents themselves didn't know the songs and that bothers me because they are part of our national DNA, of our identity. If we don't proclaim musically and verbally who we are and don't teach our kids, then it vanishes.

We still have Peaceniks emulating the peace movements of the '60s against the Vietnam War, thinking it's cool and necessary to advocate pacifism and non-violence—love, not war. Many of the adults that were Peaceniks in the '60s are saying, *Wait a minute. Back then I went to Canada rather than go to Vietnam because I didn't think our national interest was involved. But now, we've been attacked on our own soil. Thousands of Americans have been killed in New York, Washington, and Pennsylvania and we've got to do something about it.*

You can't fight that kind of terror and violence with peace slogans. You don't say to Osama bin Laden, "Please, Mr. bin Laden, we won't hold that against you, so please don't do it again. We don't want war." Can you imagine how he'd sneer at that?

There is something that is in danger of being lost. I hope its revivable in the American spirit. You don't come to our soil or attack our countrymen overseas without expecting retaliation. You just can't let hoodlums and terrorists run all over you and hope that by being peaceful and loving that's going to deter them in some way. It's not going to happen.

I've heard Dan Rather and others commenting that people are reciting the Pledge of Allegiance, saying *one nation indivisible,* leaving out *under God* in the name of political correctness, not wanting to offend anyone. The reason there is an America today is because people sought the freedom to express their faith in God and openly ask for his help. Every president we've ever had has publicly asked for the prayers of the people for their administration and for the country.

We were attacked by these madmen, these zealots, and all of a sudden there were senators and representatives on the steps of the House singing "God Bless America" and meaning it, and everybody was saying, "Yes, we need that." I didn't hear anything from the ACLU or People For the American Way. They are not representative of the true American way, which is to grant everybody the freedom to express their faith openly. Muslims, Hindus, whatever they might be, even atheists, but don't throttle and silence the great majority that want to express their faith openly, because there might be three or four people who are offended. It's a total perversion of what was intended by the framers of the Constitution, and we've let a few liberals browbeat and intimidate us into cow-towing to them.

We're either going to reclaim who we have been and who we felt we would always be, or forever lose our identity and just melt into the sea of commonality. Instead of being a role model for the world, we will become invisible like everybody else and suffer the same fate.

PART II

Chasm

David Halberstam

One of America's finest writers, Halberstam believes television
has had a tremendous effect on our culture. But with increased
competition in news, television has resorted more and more to
hype to attract listeners, to the point that the country has gone
from Calvinism, to communication, to entertainment.

In the '30s and '40s, we were a much poorer society than today. It
was much more Calvinistic. The newspapers did not devote nearly as
much space to movies, theatre, art, food. They covered politics, a little bit of sports. You worked, voted; you didn't have time for much
else. The combination of affluence and change in culture came after
the war, particularly with certain technological inventions.

The coming of such great affluence produced disposable income.
People before 1945, particularly during the Depression, didn't talk of
disposable income. You didn't go to restaurants, possibly you went to
a movie once in a while, but there wasn't a vast, broad, surging middle class with a lot of disposable income.

I believe the culture began to change in the '60s with the new affluence, more people coming into the middle class, the coming of television. There's a moment in the mid-'50s when Elvis Presley appears
and kids begin buying these little record players for 45 records and
they put them in their rooms and have their own music.

Ed Sullivan decides that Elvis's music is dirty. He's not going to have
him on his program. He boasts about this. Then Elvis goes on the rival
show, the "Steve Allen Show," gets record ratings, at which point Ed
Sullivan capitulates, almost like a politician capitulating to an aware-
ness of a new constituency, and signs Elvis for three appearances.
They shoot him at first above the waist, but it's a breakthrough.

It's about the growth of the youth economy that the traditional
forces in the economy, the hierarchy, can no longer hold back.
Television is a new source of power and the political leadership, even

57

the church leadership, and older people in their 50s and 60s can't stop the new forces which represent a great new popularity.

It begins somewhat with the coming of Rock 'n' Roll and Elvis. It's a sign that television touches and empowers new constituencies. You see this throughout the '60s, with an undeclared and rather unpopular war that doesn't work and people go into the streets to protest and television covers it.

Brown v. Board of Education in effect gave a green light to what would become the civil rights movement. It was the green light for the media to start covering race in America. What it effectively said, just beyond ending school segregation, was that segregation was wrong and therefore anything related to segregation was a legitimate target for the national media.

Television was just beginning to come on, the country was beginning to be wired nationally, and among the first beneficiaries was the civil rights movement. You got a touch of it locally in Montgomery with Rosa Parks. There was a new television station in Montgomery, and a man named Frank McGee, a very good tough guy, worked for them and he covered it.

In the South, local papers that were owned by segregationist publishers, with segregationist editors and segregationist reporters, blacked out or whited out, I guess you should say, what blacks were doing, their protests and dissent. The local newspapers had, in conjunction with the local power structure, been able to block and minimize any kind of protest. Now when they tried to do that, the blacks would go to the television station; a very important change locally.

By 1957, and embryonically in Little Rock, you had the coming of national television. Someone like John Chancellor going down there and putting the Little Rock school crisis on television. For the first time it showed the price being paid by the country in order to have segregation.

It ended the lie that Southern segregationists had put forth that black people liked being separate, liked having bad schools, liked not being able to vote. The blacks didn't know it was going to happen. It was a surprise, but they discovered that television was an ally in this struggle.

King began to deliberately chose the worst segregationist strongholds—Bull O'Connor, George Wallace, places in Mississippi—knowing that if black civil rights protestors went in there the white leadership would overreact. There would be violence. The black hats would be worn by the white racist leadership and the black protestors would be wearing the white hats. You'd have a morality play that would work for the protestors, [with] the rest of the country watching in embarrassment, which is exactly what happens.

That pace began to speed up beginning with the sit-ins, the freedom rides, and ended with the beatings in Alabama and Mississippi, culminating in the Voting Rights Act in '65. From Rosa Parks in '55, to the Voting Rights Act in '65, you have ten years, much of it heavily covered by television, in which more was accomplished for civil rights than in the previous 100 years.

There's a vast part of the black population that is not absorbed into America. There are two black populations: approximately two-thirds form an embryonic black middle class, and a third live in the inner cities and have not been absorbed and form a hard-core underclass.

By and large they come from the deep South, grew up in neo-slavery, moved to the North during the last twenty or thirty years when entry level jobs allowed blacks to get into the middle class—working in small factories, meat packing houses and such.

Now those jobs are gone, and the only jobs available are as parking attendants and such and the black family has begun to fragment at an increasing rate. You end up with bad homes, bad schools, broken family structures, and almost all the indexes of dysfunction—lack of education, drugs, homes without male heads of families—all these things are very much part of the inner city and the source of our most negative social statistics.

In the last fifty years we have become a middle class society. We've become more affluent, have a higher personal level of freedom than ever before, lead better lives. We're also for the first time accepting the fact that we're a much more diverse society. I think that's a good thing. We're enormously energized. We expect Maine, Southern California, Oregon, Washington, and Florida to have more that unites them than divides them. We are volatile yet enormously strong, constantly changing and adapting, and our strengths are not to be underestimated.

We are not going to be a white country anymore. We're going to be blended and I have great confidence. When my grandfather came here about 120 years ago a lot of people didn't think he was going to be a good citizen. He and the people like him who came from

Eastern Europe experienced all kinds of prejudice for what they represented.

Would they be good Americans? They were good Americans. They were very, very good Americans. His son fought in two wars, his grandson won the Pulitzer Prize, and two of his grandsons went to Harvard. He turned out to be a good citizen. If you look at that wall in Washington with the names of the Vietnam dead, there aren't that many pure white, Anglo-Saxon, Protestant, old-American names on it.

Alice Spearman

Alice Spearman has been an activist since age 11. She believes blacks are not respected because whites and other racial and ethnic groups in America believe they are irresponsible.

When I was 11, I went with my mother to Montgomery Ward in Oakland. We were in the parking lot and she told me to stay in the car, but I noticed people protesting in front of Montgomery Ward. I told her I was going to go see what they were doing and ended up on the protest line.

They were protesting because Montgomery Ward was not hiring blacks. At the time, most of the black people were shopping at Montgomery Ward but you couldn't be waited on by a black person.

My parents were educators and progressive people. During the black movement they were doing a lot of voter registration work down South. My mother had friends that were high up in SNCC [Student Nonviolent Coordinating Committee] and she let me go with them down South to do voter registration, to see what was going on in the civil rights movement.

I was 14, in Yazoo, Mississippi. It was a Sunday evening, at dusk, and I was told to get in the trunk of a car. There had been a lot of threats. The Ku Klux Klan was there. Three of us were stuck in the trunk of the car and taken out of Yazoo, Mississippi, for our safety. Later I found out it was the Ku Klux Klan and they had targeted the folks that had come in to help the community with this voter registration.

We had a right to vote. They didn't have the right to ask us to do any kind of exit exam or anything like that. My mother sent me to experience the racism, to find out I couldn't ride just anywhere on the bus. I was told very clearly how to speak, who to speak to.

I went to Cuba in 1969. A group of us flew to Puerto Rico, and through Puerto Rico we went into Cuba to be with comrades. We wanted to experience collectivism, socialism, to find out about the revolution, to be around people of the revolution. It was very difficult. Very difficult. I came from a family that did a lot of camping and roughing it, but I wasn't prepared to live in an environment that didn't have hot and cold running water, heaters, and stoves. I was there three days.

The people were lovely. The experience with the group was good. I didn't stay long enough to find out if I could have lived in that type of society—what we would call the bush in Africa.

The cultural side of the black movement dealt with knowing who you are. Knowing your past, knowing Africa. Living a different life and to live separately. I've always been around African-American groups that talked about having a self-contained society, a self-contained community where we ran the grocery stores, ran the dry goods stores, took care of ourselves, where we were self-sufficient.

People in this country still perceive black people as descendants of slaves. That we have no capacity for education, have no capacity to run the country. That we do not have the capacity to do anything but take drugs, drink, and have a bunch of babies. We're lazy. We don't want to work and we're not motivated to do anything. That's the stereotypical thinking of cash America. They see that before they see anything else about you.

Statistics reveal black men in corporate America make significantly less than their white counterparts doing the same job, that black women make less than white women in the same job.

Even though we think we've crossed the barrier, it has not been crossed.

Why are our children still failing in school? Why are they not receiving the same benefits as everyone else? Our children are further behind now than they've ever been.

White teachers indoctrinate our children to make them think they can't achieve. And no matter how hard they try, they will still be in the same bucket.

You cannot be black and be a CEO of a major company. It's not so much the color of your skin, it is your thoughts and mind-set. That when you "arrive" you have to play "fair." You cannot bring on your black brothers and sisters because that's not right. That's not "fair."

I believe [the educational problems] are more the fault of the family than the educational system. But for a long time during the '70s and early '80s, we had a lot of high school dropouts, we had a lot of teenage mothers and people who had some very poor experiences in education. This is where the perception that if you do well, you are a traitor to your race started.

There are mixed emotions about Colin Powell. A lot of African-Americans do not respect him as an African-American. He says he's from Jamaica, or from the islands, so he is letting you know *I was not born here, I'm not of here*. Also he's a Republican. I also think Colin has just as much black in him as any other African-American, but he has a different ring on politics. But that doesn't make him a traitor.

I think much was accomplished in the late '50s and the '60s in civil rights. The accomplishments began to decline in the late '70s and '80s. It happened because a lot of us Baby Boomers took advantage of the educational system, got into decent jobs, and then we became a little bit complacent.

But also [we became] a bit materialistic and decided we were going to make it better for our children. We forgot about home and we worked and didn't pay enough attention to our children. The individualism came in and not the collectivism.

If it wasn't for the Black Panthers and SNCC we wouldn't have had an impact at all. The Panther Party, SNCC, they pushed 'em, they pushed them. They pushed the movement.

We're not going to wait any longer. We're going to take it. We're going to stand up. It's ours. We're black and we're proud. We will protect ourselves. We will be self-sufficient. We will not wait for this country to give us anything. Forget about giving us something. We'll do for ourselves.

The Culturalists were a group and the New African Republic was one of them. They mostly examined culture and history. Had it not been for them we would not have known where we came from, where we had to go: as far as being African, descendants of Africans, knowing what the continent of Africa was about. About the people, about the cultures, the society that reigned in Africa for hundreds of thousands of years and to be proud of being who we were.

You weren't just in one place. Some people were very committed to the New African Republic. Some people were very committed to SNCC. Some were very committed to the Panther Party. And then some people moved in different circles because you had to be well-rounded.

Most of our major leaders at this time came out of the Southern Christian Leadership. The Congress of Racial Equality produced a few.

The non-violent group started first. They were the first ones out. They were the first ones to put their lives on the line. By putting their lives on the line, it rooted a religious belief and many of us decided we weren't turning the cheek. You hit me, I'm hitting you back. Threaten me, I'm going to protect myself.

I think white society decided to make laws to put us in prison. If I stand up for my rights, or I'm too aggressive, too assertive, if I threaten somebody, I lose my job. If I'm stopped by the police and it is unwarranted, if I say anything, I go to jail. My children are harassed a lot by police. They have decided to acknowledge *driving while black*. It doesn't matter what age or sex you are. It has always been here. Now it's being acknowledged.

One of the good things is the knowledge we, as African-Americans, were the forerunners of everyone's civil rights. Now you see gays, people of different sexual persuasions, using the same tactics. More so now, you are seeing other people of color, other cultures doing the same thing. But what's really strange is they exclude us because they've been indoctrinated to think black people are nothing, that everyone is better than a black person.

I've seen children and adults of different cultures tell us we're not [anything]. That everything that comes into this country is better than an African-American.

This country says the institution of slavery was illegal and wrong. They apologize for it and do everything to make sure it never happens again. We have a lot of people saying they don't owe us nothing. But you do. That was our great-grandfathers and grandfathers.

There's not enough money to pay for the suffering the black people have endured for over 400 years. There is no compensation that will pay for the pain. However, there is a feeling in some African-American communities that monetary compensation will be acceptable.

I would like to leave it up to a group to decide and then ask us and see what most of the folks would like to accept, if that's what they want. Put it in a general fund like they did for the Japanese and the Jewish people. The Jewish people and the Japanese are still receiving reparations. The Japanese were put in concentration camps—supposedly they were Americans.

When they wrote the Constitution, we were never considered a whole person—it's still there. Even though the Fifteenth Amendment gave us the right to vote, they never repealed where we were less than two-thirds of a man. As long as you have this hanging on, legislatively, until they change that, there's no healing going to occur. And my folks have to heal.

We are going to survive and we're going to survive dutifully and willfully. We are not going anywhere. You can't move us out of the country and we're going to succeed.

Terry Anderson

Anderson is a product of the '60s. He served in Vietnam, then entered college and joined the protest movement. Now a professor of history at Texas A&M and an expert on the period, he has written *The Movement* and *The '60s*. Terry believes the Vietnam War radicalized the student movement, the Tet Offensive being the turning point, and that in the end the kids won.

In the early 1960s, things were coming together: Kennedy idealism and the civil rights movement were asking all kinds of important questions, such as what rights do Negro Americans have, as they were then called. They didn't have any rights whatsoever.

White, middle class kids went down South in the summer of 1964, picketed, marched, and got involved in the civil rights movement, then went back to college in the fall and discovered they had few rights on their own campuses. They had rules and regulations no student today would abide by.

They had free speech regulations which denied the First Amendment on college campuses such as Berkeley, Indiana University, and Ohio State. Institutions talked about the freedom of ideas, how horrible communism and the Soviet Union were, at the same time not allowing certain speakers on their campuses and editing out anything that didn't seem patriotic or complimentary regarding the university.

A number of students saw this great inconsistency and began to march and demand their rights as American citizens. They were of draft age but were denied their rights on a college campus. Most people thought that was preposterous and they confronted the deans and in the long run they won.

I discount particular individuals of the student movement and discount most of the organizations because without the student body behind them they would have had three people picketing and would not have even been a thorn in the side of the administrations.

The free speech movement is important in Berkeley, and its ideas were picked up by college papers in 1964 and 1965 and spread across the country. Institutions in 1967 were re-evaluating their regulations such as hours for male and female visitation in dorm rooms. The result was by 1968 almost all public universities had abolished their *in loco parentis* rules and regulations and allowed free speech and gave more input to the student body.

The war is the engine of the 1960s. The war fuels virtually everything and eventually radicalizes all of the movements because the war is long and frustrating. People get sick and tired of the war and it makes all of the movements more radical because we're not winning and we're not getting out. After Tet in 1968, Americans realize *hey, the government's been lying. We're not going to be able to get out of this war.* The rhetoric from the Johnson Administration in the fall of 1967 that we can see the light at the end of the tunnel and the enemy's hopes are bankrupt was nonsense.

The emperor had no clothes, so when are we going to get out? Everybody thought Johnson, by not running for president in 1968, would get out [of the war]. But of course we weren't going to get out. What we got was Nixon. His peace-with-honor program was another four years of the war. People had been out protesting the war for a number of years and it was going to be a very slow withdrawal— Vietnamization—the result more frustration and more violent antics.

The first of the violent acts begins about 1967 against Dow Chemical. Dow Chemical is holding interviews at the University of Wisconsin and students are trying to shut the interviews down because Dow Chemical is the maker of napalm, and they call in the University police force and start swinging clubs. This horrifies most of the student body and, of course, you get an immediate chasm between people who think the police are right and those who think the police are wrong.

People at the statehouse in Madison yell for the kids to be expelled; professors and students yell for the police to be fired, and that's just the first of many.

Nixon provoked Kent State by sending troops into Cambodia after eighteen months of saying he was winding down the war, the result being the horrible deaths of four students in Kent, Ohio. Then hundreds of campuses absolutely explode and half a dozen governors have to call in the National Guard. You have this incredible gap between the silent majority and the youth movement of the country.

Chicago was the first time there was a major confrontation between the authorities and radical students. In August of 1968 you had a bunch of people—Yippies, SDS, and a number of other groups and organizations—who are going to be right in the face of the police. They're going to do whatever they can to provoke these people.

You didn't do that, that wasn't the way people behaved in America, and now all of a sudden these foul-mouthed, long-haired kids are yelling things at the police, whom you're supposed to respect, calling them things like "pig." The flash point was very low with the Chicago police, the result being a police riot in which they just ran amuck.

The vast majority of Chicago residents supported the police. You can read the editorials—which I have—that say, *Why don't you hit them harder, we don't like this kind of behavior, they are not our children, these are outside agitators.*

If you were against the war, you were a communist. Your dad wouldn't talk to you because he was probably a World War II or Korean War vet, and everyone always supported the government. But in 1968 people were saying, "Well, we're not going to support it any more. This is a lost cause."

The student movement almost had a total victory. All the colleges that were public institutions got rid of *in loco parentis* rules and regulations and gave much more freedom of the press to the daily student newspapers. Gave students more choices relative to their classes. Got rid of most of the dorm rules.

The amount of freedom kids have on campus today is taken for granted. When they read my book to see what it was like in 1963 and 1964, they're just absolutely appalled. *Dress codes? You mean you had dress codes?*

Students have more freedom on campus than they've ever had, not only in curriculum but in the types of regulations, so they won the cause. As far as the civil rights movement was concerned, there were massive changes resulting in the 1964 Civil Rights Act, the 1965 Voting Rights Act, the 1968 Fair Housing Rights Act, and the establishment of affirmative action. So there were many gains.

The anti-war movement forced one president to quit and not run again. It forced the country to seek ways out of the war. In the November 1968 election, the only person who's supporting increasing the war effort is George Wallace, and he gets 13 percent of the vote.

Everybody else is thinking about a way out of the war and so we elect a man who says *peace with honor* because that's the handiest slogan at the time and he has a secret plan to get us out of the war.

He immediately starts withdrawing, but it was a very slow and painful four-year withdrawal, but he knew what he had to do. He had to get most of those troops out by the time he was going for re-election and that's exactly what he did. If there had not been an anti-war movement, I believe Richard Nixon would have kept fighting Ho Chi Minh's communism for many more years. The anti-war movement, although frustrated and becoming more radical all the time, basically forced the government to re-evaluate the war and to get out of a situation which most Americans, after 1968 and Tet, did not think was in our national interest.

These kids wanted to be able to vote, and [they] got the 18-year-old vote. They wanted to get rid of the draft, and did, getting an all-volunteer service. They moved into environmental issues. They moved into women's liberation, the result being the most successful social movement in the history of the American Republic—women's liberation.

They fundamentally altered the way we deal with the sexes. You look at want ads today. It doesn't say male and female any more, does it?

Paul Major

During the 1960s, Major was a hippie, a "druggie," and a disc jockey at the first "Underground" radio station in the country—KMPX. The audience were known as hippy freaks, their music consisting of Janis Joplin, Jimmy Hendrix, Jefferson Airplane, and a host of other counter-culture individuals and groups. The audience—seldom large—felt the music was theirs, that it brought others like them together to form a community, that finally they had a voice.

The first big music event was the Monterey Pop Festival in June 1967. By this time the Haight was established, a number of people were being called *hippies*, although we never called ourselves that. This was an invention by Herb Caen, who also coined the name *beatniks*.

The Grateful Dead, Jefferson Airplane, and Quicksilver Messenger Service were the three main groups. They were the first ones to get contracts with recording companies, so our neighborhood music was becoming widespread.

I remember the first time I listened to something and knew there was a drug lyric involved. This may surprise you, but it was a song called "Elusive Butterfly" by Bob Lind about 1966. There's a line in there . . .*take me disappearing through the canyons of your mind.* Anybody who had ever done LSD knew exactly what that was like. It was an identification that we recognized.

I knew a lot of people who came out of folk rather than '50s Rock 'n' Roll, which we disdained. It was nice history, though not really relevant, but interesting to hear Chuck Berry and some of those guys who got it on in the '50s and early '60s.

We all identified with MoTown. Of course, there was no drug-related stuff on MoTown, but it was wonderful music to listen and dance to.

The Monterey Pop Festival started out as a promotion for the Mamas and Papas put on by John Phillips to highlight the group. They appeared the first night, along with Simon and Garfunkel, and it got a pretty good reception. The second day they got the underground groups like Big Brother, The Airplane, The Dead, Country Joe McDonald, and the first American appearance of the Jimmy Hendrix Experience. The Who, not well known yet, were there.

It was quite an event, very peaceful. People were pinning roses on the police and everybody was smiling and happy. It was wonderful and that was the first and last one like that. After that came Altamont and other troubles.

About six months later, a new paper came out called *Rolling Stone*. This was our bible. This was OUR magazine. This belonged to us. It was in San Francisco. All the people involved in it were San Francisco people. We knew them, socialized with them. I remember the first issue had a whole thing about what happened to the money from Monterey Pop because somehow or other it couldn't be accounted for and it was all supposed to go to wonderful charities. I don't know what became of that, whether it ever did get accounted for and distributed.

That was the beginning of the periodicals, the magazines, the chronicling of that time. It started in November '67 and grew very rapidly. Our people were becoming famous. There weren't that many drug inferences at the beginning. The Airplane was very folksy, very pretty stuff for the most part. The Grateful Dead was basically a bluegrass band when they started. A lot of people don't know that, but when they became so country later, you could look back and see where it started.

KMPX was the radio station—the country's first underground station. Underground radio is not exactly what people think it is today. You could play anything you wanted. People would listen because we were really good at tying songs together. It was our trip. I remember going there the second night the station was on the air as rock and going wild. This was it. This was the music I wanted to hear.

Then KSAN was started. It was an independent, and later became part of Metromedia. Most of the listenership went over there.

Tom Donohoe took the format and made it viable so they could actually sell it to advertisers. It was '60s Rock 'n' Roll, a lot of folk music, a lot of blues. People were coming along like Van Morrison.

It's still wonderful to me. There was never a play list. We didn't even keep track of what we played. Sometimes we didn't back announce, which was unprofessional, but that's how it was.

There were stations in L.A., Boston, and New York. KZAP in Sacramento started. Unfortunately, none of these were ever big advertising successes. They had a loyal audience, but it wasn't huge. You could not go out and sell Chevrolet on the station.

It was *join us* and be in the *in crowd*. It wasn't so much that they had drugs in their lyrics. The Grateful Dead were probably as big a drug band as there was, but there wasn't much in there about drugs. The biggest drug thing . . . somebody talked about marijuana, but very rarely. "Puff the Magic Dragon" was not a marijuana song. We laughed.

William Safire thought that a Jefferson Airplane was when you bent a match in half to hold a joint to smoke it down. We thought that was the most hilarious thing in the world because the group came from a totally different place. They were followers of Blindlem Jefferson Airplane and they just became Jefferson Airplane,

If we were at the Filmore or the Avalon or one of those places, there was going to be drugs all over the place. Everybody would be high, but everybody was reasonably peaceful. I remember the wonderful things that Bill Graham used to do. I remember New Year's Eve '66-'67 when they had the Airplane, the Dead, and Quicksilver. They played from eight at night until six in the morning and then he served a full breakfast, all for five bucks. I've still got the poster of that one.

Different kinds of drugs came in. The original drug culture, at least as far as San Francisco was concerned, was psychedelics and marijuana . . . and a lot of wine. By the end of '67, speed began to show up. It's a different kind of drug and puts you in a different frame of mind and tends to be on the violent side. That's when things really began to change.

Most of the original hippies were out of San Francisco by the end of '67. They saw where things were going and it wasn't peace-love-dope anymore. It was get the money and do whatever you had to do to get it. A lot of those people vanished up into Sonoma and Mendocino counties.

Underground radio was a community. That was our station. *Rolling Stone* was our newspaper. We could fall by the station anytime we wanted, say hello, sit there all night if we wanted, or all day. We could fall by *Rolling Stone* and meet people and talk. It was just very much a community. I'm only talking San Francisco, because that's my experience.

That gradually began to go away. By the time *Rolling Stone* moved to New York in the '70s, they were all suits, lured by the big money.

Dope was never a problem in San Francisco. People were giving it away in the early days. I remember walking down Haight Street and a person I only vaguely knew said, "Open wide." I did, and he put in a hit of LSD, smiling all the time. This was different. The corporate culture did not deal with it well.

I think a lot of people started very innocently hanging out with the bands and smoking dope and taking psychedelics. I didn't see anybody shooting anything in the '60s. First time I remember was a good friend of mine. I went over to his house and he was shooting speed. I was shocked. I hadn't seen anything like that. That drug changed things.

With marijuana you don't want to get up and do anything. As long as you've got a 55-pound bag of Oreos, you're happy. The idea of that being a violent drug was absurd.

We knew the government was lying to us. Vietnam vets were coming back and telling us what really went on over there. We knew they lied to us about some drugs, so we assumed they lied to us about all the drugs. If you say marijuana is a violent drug, we know better than that. So when they said speed is a violent drug, we didn't pay any attention.

Frank Zappa in the '60s was saying speed kills on his records. He wasn't talking about driving too fast. There were a lot of anti-drug messages from people. Hoyt Axton and Goddamn The Pusher Man. It wasn't all pro. People were seeing problems with the different types of drugs that were coming in.

I saw a lot of the results, a lot of speed freaks, a lot of people who if predisposed were going to be involved in it for a long time. I was. I had a predisposition to alcohol and drugs. I already had enough of an alcohol problem when I hit San Francisco in '66. A lot of people never got away from it. I remember one guy at the radio station joined Alcoholics Anonymous in 1970 and we thought he was nuts. I mean, what are you talking about? You don't drink anymore than I do.

I didn't see much heroin. I know it was around. Janis Joplin was pretty heavily into heroin. A lot of people became dealers and a lot of people who were users made it available. It scared the hell out of me, and I didn't do it. There's never been a time since Bayer invented it in 1898 that heroin has not been around.

The Vietnam War was one of the biggest factors in the use of drugs. So many guys came back from there addicted to heroin and other drugs. It's said that over 70 percent of the homeless are Vietnam vets. Not that they don't want to work. They can't. They're damaged. And, of course, Reagan turned them all out into the streets as governor.

We became very suspicious of our government, which I'm not sure is a bad thing. We found out people were lying to us and we thought perhaps all of them were—that kind of distrust. We placed a great deal of value in the truth, whatever it might be. We did not want to be lied to.

I look back on it with nostalgia, as do many people. I see a lot of problems that started there and I see a lot of good things that started there. It's difficult to put a blanket indictment or a blanket approval on the '60s. It was a very turbulent time. We lost a president, a possible president, and Martin Luther King to violence, and that scared the hell out of many of us. Many quit participating in the system, seeing it wasn't working.

Many look back at the '60s thinking it was an interesting time, glad we were there, and don't want to see it happen again.

Bill Stirton

Stirton served in Vietnam from November 1970 to September 1971. Nixon's Vietnamization—the slow withdrawal of troops—was taking place, resulting in fewer men to fight the war. To complicate matters, there was widespread use of drugs and morale had hit bottom. Stirton's son is in the Navy, commissioned to attend flight school thirty-one years after his father received his commission. Bill is very proud of him and believes his son's generation is the next "greatest generation."

When I got to Vietnam, they took the lowest-level officers who had artillery training and assigned them to an infantry company. Your job was to handle the direction of the artillery and call in naval gunfire and other fire support for the infantry. I was a forward observer.

In the mid-'60s, forward observers didn't live very long. That's why they sent three artillery people out at a time. Anybody with a map or radio was a target. By the time I got there there was less of that, but they still had a very short life expectancy.

We had some bad experiences with the South Vietnamese Army. One time we were assigned a project working with the ARVNs, which is the Republic of Vietnam Army. The Viet Cong lobbed a big artillery round at us and it went off in front of our perimeter and they just packed up and went home. It was that kind of war for them because they knew it was going to be there tomorrow. We were going home in a year for the most part, but they were going to stay there. We could not rely on them in situations where we needed their support. You certainly couldn't count on them to help you.

We did get some help. We had Korean troops who were first class. We were always excited if we could work near them because we knew they would protect us. Australia had some troops, but I never had any contact with them. They were well respected as well.

I arrived in 1970 and Nixon had begun Vietnamization and we were turning the war over to the Vietnamese. For example, we were

assigned to the DMZ up at the patrol bases for about six weeks while
the Vietnamese troops went to Khe Sahn to engage the enemy in a
full-scale battle. Many of our missions were just going into the countryside and trying to find some enemy location that our intelligence
people told us was out there.

When I was there the war was more a mental thing, more psycho-
logical than fighting full-scale battles. We would be assigned to patrol
certain areas of the countryside and our biggest enemies were mines
and booby-traps because the Viet Cong would certainly know where
we were and were constantly trying to find ways to send us back home.

I'd say almost everybody who was in Vietnam had some psycholog-
ical wounds of some kind that they had to deal with. What guys did
was they built a wall up and pretended nothing happened. They
needed to deal with things and it didn't surface until maybe ten years
later. This is called post-traumatic stress syndrome, which the country began to realize caused serious problems with many of the men
and women who came back from Vietnam.

I've been told that the Army when we first got there was an out-
standing group. But by the time I arrived people had grown very
tired of the war, and it was obvious the country had no intention of
trying to win it by the type of support that we were given. They were
all cynics. To motivate people at that stage—these were for the most
part drafted people and did not want to be in the Army.

There were a lot of drugs. I saw it in the field. In fact, my radio
operator had to be sent to the rear. I told him I couldn't take the risk.
It was obvious he was using cocaine or heroin or something along
those lines and it was too dangerous to have him out there. Villagers
would come and sell drugs to the troops in the field.

Drugs were suspected of being a cause when Firebase Mary Ann
was overrun in 1971. They believe the guys on the perimeter were
using drugs and weren't as alert as they should have been to the sap-
pers, who got through and overran the firebase, resulting in, as I
remember, 80 to 100 American deaths.

When I came back to the States, for the most part I didn't tell people I'd been to Vietnam. I hoped they wouldn't find out because it
seemed to make you some kind of loser, a drug addict, a baby-killer.
A lot of negative thoughts went along with people who had admitted
to being a Vietnam veteran.

The press primarily promoted the negative side of the Vietnam experience. A CBS documentary showed the Vietnam soldiers using drugs in the field on one of their missions in Cambodia. The My Lai massacre and the publicity that it received. The movies that were made. Everything seemed to promote the negative side of the Vietnam experience.

When I returned, I was in a combat zone one day, then jumped on a plane and the next day I was watching "Monday Night Football." The following day I was released from the Army. I was in a stressful situation one day, then back to a normal situation the next. You had no benefit of transitional counseling to get you readjusted to the world and you stayed quiet about what had happened to you and tried to fit in. I think most of the guys were proud of what they did, but they didn't think anybody else would agree with them so they kept quiet about it.

Most Vietnam veterans feel they were pretty well used and abused and thrown back into the pile. Although there certainly were things like the G.I. Bill, most guys don't believe they got back what they put into it.

I was not anti-war. I was there because I thought that was what my country wanted me to do. I didn't fit into the draft dodger category. I felt it was my duty to go, and when I got there I tried to make sure that my men and I survived.

Guys were young when they went over there, younger than other war veterans. The Vietnam vet averaged 19 years of age. In World War II it was 23. In Korea it was about 26. The difference in years makes a big difference in how someone handles stress. Some were not equipped to handle the pressure and some of this came out in post-traumatic stress syndrome, the high rate of suicides and criminal activities, and the high percentage of the homeless which are Vietnam veterans—estimates as high as 40 percent.

Most guys sat on it for about ten years. After that ten-year period, I knew something was wrong and I took advantage of the Outreach Program that the government set up. I went through some counseling and it helped me tremendously in realizing that there were other people who were feeling the same way I was. That what I was feeling wasn't wrong, that you could work through it and get yourself back to a more healthy mental state.

You hide your emotions. You're almost emotionless. It contributed to my first marriage not surviving. You just couldn't show emotion.

That's not good if you're trying to have a successful relationship with anybody, let alone your wife.

It makes your heart warm to see what the reaction has been to 9-11. To walk out your door and see flags flying from your neighbors' houses. It's a great feeling. In Los Angeles, to see more U.S. flags flying from cars than Laker flags, you know people have their priorities right. I have a son who was commissioned thirty-one years after I, on almost the same ground as I was commissioned, and he's going to be out there as a pilot with the Navy.

He should be flying combat in about a year and a half. I've thought about this a lot, and this is one of those wars that's going to take a long time to reach the right conclusion. So I'm sure that he's going to be out there, but he's got the right attitude.

The type of people that I see serving with my son, I'm proud of them. These kids are intelligent. Their mental and physical condition is great and they're ready to go and they feel their country's behind them. This is a much different situation than 1970 and 1971.

I can tell you firsthand my son is ready to go, and his friends in the service—they're the kind of people we had in the '40s—they won't give up. We've got the people to meet the challenges that others are bringing to us. I couldn't feel more optimistic!

Laurie

As a teenager in the1960s, she was an enthusiastic participant in the sex and drugs of that time. Her mother told her to be a "good girl," to show restraint and use common sense. But this message was in opposition to what she was hearing from the feminists: *exercise your freedom*—especially sexual freedom. The feminists won the day, but although she has no guilty feelings, she now realizes it was the wrong message.

I grew up in a Southern California beach town. Was born in the mid-'50s to a middle-class Catholic family. I went to Catholic school through ninth grade, then public high school.

The Vietnam War seemed to have everybody's attention. I began learning about drugs; drugs became a big issue. There was a lot of protesting going on, a lot of rebelliousness on all levels, including sexual. At this time I wasn't remotely interested in sex. So those things kind of just floated by. I didn't fear it, but had no desire for it. I was just too young at that time. The only message I was getting was from my mother: don't do it.

She was freaking out because of what was going on. I was coming to the age where she felt it very important to expound on the fact that I should not engage in any sexual acts until I was married. If I did engage, I would be thought of poorly, have a reputation that would ruin my life, and it was something nice girls didn't do. I don't know if my mother would have been this passionate about it if it wasn't for the times.

I heard things were changing, but because I had nothing to compare it to, I didn't have a clue. Later, when the sexual revolution was in full swing, I had no fear of sex and didn't know what the big hoopla was about. I just felt very comfortable about it, very free. It didn't move me one way or the other, but that's because I was so young and hadn't known the joys of it.

I became interested in sex at 16. Active when I was about 18.

Everybody was doing it. If you were going out to party it was nothing for your friends to go off and have sex and come back and join the party. And it didn't have to be in the context of a relationship. In fact, that was somewhat ridiculous at our age.

Drugs came in and out of the whole thing. But I wouldn't connect the whole sex thing with drugs. I'd connect it more with alcohol because alcohol, in my experience, lowered my inhibitions where drugs didn't. Depending on the drug, it would make me paranoid and self-conscious. My inhibitions weren't lowered enough to really go into that free flow of sex.

The more potent drugs were a lot more fun than sex. It could have been because I wasn't fully active. I was still so young. I didn't know what everybody was making such a big deal about. I don't know if I was influenced by the energy that was going around, or would have felt that way had there not been a sexual revolution.

I was affected by the media. The messages I was getting were from magazines for girls a little bit older than myself. They were really supporting the feminist movement, women's rights. Our right to choose, our right to say no. Our right to have birth control and screw around as much as we wished. The message I got was from the rising feminist movement, which was still in its real early days. The real radicals were not there yet.

I wasn't that interested in the music. It was lyric driven. A lot of it was about drugs and acid trips. Jefferson Airplane did a great song called "White Rabbit" about a psychedelic drug trip and Jimmy Hendrix did things as well, as did Janis Joplin—drug related. I actually liked older music such as Chuck Berry, R&B, old Rock 'n' Roll.

Our country was in such an upheaval. The war had tons to do with it. There was a lot of fear. A lot of kids who got involved in drugs were preparing to go to war. It was just atrocious what was going on. I think people were looking for answers and explanations in a world that couldn't provide them. Some people overdid it, more boys than girls. I don't remember too many girls being wasted from drugs.

Looking back on it, I am sure I had a better time than my parents did. They grew up during the Depression and the War. I had it a lot easier, had more fun, more freedom. What saddens me is I see now that the '60s, '70s era hurt families; hurt the values, morals, and ethics that people grew up and lived by.

My parents tried to instill it in me, but I didn't embrace it. It didn't become my truth or my reality; again it was the times. I was part of it and it psychically trashed our generation. It broke down the disciplines which were important for people to have in their lives.

I think my generation did achieve some things on a positive level. I wouldn't have the expanded mind and the acceptance I have today had I grown up at any other time, and I'm really grateful for that. I'm grateful I can look at things without judgment. Growing up in those times made me less narrow-minded than my mother's generation.

People need structure. Children need it, and it saddens me to see how we allowed it to be cheapened to where it doesn't matter. I don't know if we can get that back. I was at the pivot point where the culture was changing. My son is in his early 20s and came into the world we have today. Drugs are not a new thing, sex is not a new thing. Single parent families are not new. This is the world he knows. He knows no other.

How did your mother handle this?

She took tranquilizers. She took her own drugs.

My mother still believes the feminist movement, drugs, and the sexual revolution destroyed America. Remember, she grew up in another time, but I agree with her.

As a result of the feminist movement, men were placed in a precarious position. They didn't know their place. There were no longer roles, nor structure. As a result of women stepping out of their roles, it changed men's roles and weakened them. It made them angry. Men can't be men because women aren't being women. That's not the way it's set up to be and we're seeing the repercussions of that, especially in the family.

The feminist movement was as radical as anything that was going on. As radical as the war, as radical as the drug problem. It vibrated at the same frequency.

We had an insane war that made no sense. Our children were being killed. Atrocities were being committed. We had drug problems that were killing people, destroying their lives, destroying families. We had the sexual revolution destroying families. There were no values, and it was an intense period.

By the time the feminist movement was in full swing, I really wasn't interested. I was more interested in having fun. Little bit of drugs, little bit of sex. A lot of freedom of choice. The part I took from the feminist movement was the freedom of choice, but the price was too high. I think it's very sad.

George Will

Will, author, columnist, and television commentator, believes the 1950s was an important decade that helped define the 1960s. He contends that the activists lost the '60s because Nixon won in 1968, that the Great Society bred a moral poverty that is with us today, and that the liberation of the '60s had to do with taking drugs and developing victimization skills among other things.

The 1950s, although supposedly quiet, were obviously pregnant with the 1960s. The '60s had to come from somewhere. I have always believed that the first great protest movement of the 1960s was from the right, and it began in Chicago at the Republican Convention when the junior senator from Arizona went to the podium and said, *Conservatives, if you want to take back this party, and I think you can, let's get on with it.* That was Barry Goldwater.

The idea that the 1950s was a quiet and boring time is as out of date as the view that Dwight Eisenhower was an incompetent, bumbling president. Eisenhower, who had dealt with Churchill, Roosevelt, DeGaulle, and Stalin, was quite a sophisticated wielder of executive power.

The 1950s were a reticent decade. People had fought and won the war, had experienced the Depression. They were business-like, sober adults. The great reversal was the moral exhibitionism of the 1960s.

The Baby Boomers had a critical mass in the sense they could produce their own economy, their own cultural expressions—Rock 'n' Roll particularly. They had enough spending money that the economy turned to serve them. They had a sense of identity because of their sheer size, and as a result they became self-absorbed and developed a sense of entitlement.

But the everydayness of domestic life did catch up with them. But even when they were radical, they weren't very radical. They were radicals on credit cards, radicals in cushy college dorms. It was a radicalism of an extremely privileged group. It was a radicalism born of a mild threat to that privilege, which was conscription. And the Vietnam protests, of course, began to wither as the draft calls began to wither.

What did they do? They had this genuinely radical period in the mid-'60s and in 1968, but what was the consequence? Richard Nixon and George Wallace between them got a substantial majority of the votes. So if the radicals moved the country at all, they moved it to the right in reaction.

Essentially, there had been no liberal legislating majority in Congress since the 1938 election put the brakes on the New Deal. Roosevelt had overreached with his court-packing plan and the country reacted against him. Between 1938 and the anti-Goldwater landslide in '64, conservative Democrats, combined with Republicans, were able to stop any serious lurch to the left.

For two years, but only two years, between the 1964 election and the 1966 correction in the off-year elections, Johnson had pretty much his own way and proceeded with his Great Society.

Sargent Shriver, who was head of the War on Poverty for Lyndon Johnson, was asked by a Congressional committee how long it would take to eliminate poverty in America. Sarge said ten years. Now that made a certain sense if poverty was what poverty was then understood to be. Trouble is it wasn't. It had changed.

The old idea of poverty was that poor people are just like everyone else except they lack certain material goods and services the government knows how to deliver—transportation, jobs, housing, education, etc. But that was changing, and the signal of this change occurred in 1965 when two lines on a graph crossed in a way that was ominous. One line was the declining line of unemployment, and the intersecting line was the simultaneously rising line of welfare dependency.

That wasn't supposed to happen, but it did. And what that signaled was that we had a new kind of poverty. It was behavioral poverty. Moral and spiritual poverty, if you will. A poverty driven by the fact that a certain class of people lacked the habits, mores, customs, values, dispositions, and ideas necessary to prosper.

In fact, they were so passive the government almost felt it had no choice but to sustain them. We have changed. Our great social project is liberation. Liberation from all restraints. Liberation from rules—not just from laws—but from inner restraints as well. The therapeutic ethic that says the confessional nature of public discourse where people present themselves as victims set upon by external forces is superior to reticence.

Jim Clarke

Clarke, a very successful attorney in Chicago, was born in 1949. Therefore demographically he is a Baby Boomer. That is as far as it goes, though. Failing to conform to their unconformity when he was younger, he sees them continuing to cling to their alternate versions of history and self-absorbed existences.

The Baby Boomers were born between '46 and '65, which is an awfully broad demographic group. I have read that the name has something to do with the pent-up libidos of soldiers returning from the war, but that is a little too vivid for me to think about.

Twenty years seems like an awfully long period to define a generation. Having been born in '49, I don't feel a unique kinship with someone born in 1965, who wasn't even alive when President Kennedy was shot. If there was a seminal public event for my generation, that might be it. You had to be just the right age to accept Camelot at face value and then be truly staggered and terrified when it ended.

Obviously, the Boomers do not all conform to the stereotype. It would not be surprising to learn that a majority of us do not. In a big publicly held corporation, someone who owns 15 percent of the stock can often control the corporation as a practical matter. The remaining 85 percent is usually so disorganized, so fragmented, that 15 percent pulling together can accomplish almost anything and determine corporate policy and how the corporation is perceived by the world.

The same is true of the Baby Boomers. Not everybody is the same, but there is this group that conforms to the stereotype of the rock music, the clothing, the politics, the speech, and they have pretty much set the standard for the rest of us. It is not a difficult standard to live up to, but it's not one I'm very comfortable with anyway.

Rock music is probably the single biggest defining characteristic that comes to mind, and I remember back in the mid-'50s when Elvis

Presley evoked disdain from our elders, which seemed reason enough to follow him. After that, I fell off the train.

I wasn't interested in the majority—I certainly wasn't obsessed with the music that came afterwards as many people were. The Beatles were to me a modestly talented quartet. But if you say that to most of my contemporaries, you're treated with outrage, hostility. It's a mortal sin to blaspheme the Beatles.

It's best to pussyfoot around it and offer no opinion because anything short of adoration is unacceptable. The harder the music, the closer to absolute hard metal, the more it's revered by a subset and the less penetrable it is to the rest of us. So it's best not to even think about it.

But if you have a somewhat traditional sensibility about these things, you remember a time, like the rest of human history, when singing, screeching, whining, snarling, and yelling were distinct activities. Now they're all run together. You might like the way a certain person snarls, but I suspect sixty years ago no one would have said that that person was singing. They would have said he's snarling well. There is certainly a lot of mainstream rock music in which no one even arguably sings in the traditional sense of that word.

Our very high-minded generation that espouses ideals from universal peace on down nevertheless identifies with astonishingly idiotic television programs such as "Gilligan's Island," "The Partridge Family," "The Brady Bunch." You see these people on quiz shows and they can tell you Mrs. Brady's third cousin's maiden name. And they think that's important.

Are those shows any more insipid than "Ozzie and Harriet"? Probably not, but you don't see many people carrying a torch for "Ozzie and Harriet." Those of us who can remember the neighbor on "Ozzie and Harriet" was named "Thorny" don't make a big deal of it and don't expect anybody else to care.

We've gone through so many remarkably bad fads, including bell bottoms and tie-dyed everything. It was almost inevitable that they hit on something that was right, and of course there's nothing innovative about it. Our friend the farmer came up with blue jeans, which are a wonderful, universal sort of leveling garment. It's almost like the American Mao suit or something. If everybody can wear it, everybody starts off being equal.

It is a very old observation that people who would level society are never interested in bringing lower people up to their level. They're interested in boosting themselves upward. Blue jeans or no blue jeans, nobody really was inviting the unwashed to their party or anyone beneath them.

I remember one of my classmates in college was a very well-to-do kid from Philadelphia. He'd gone to prep school, had all the right social credentials, and he arrived at Harvard in the fall of '67 driving his Austin Healy and wearing his cutting-edge wardrobe. He took in the political atmosphere of the day which, of course, was suffused with all the feelings of the Vietnam War era and decided that the Austin Healy was not the right image and his wardrobe wasn't quite the thing.

He did not, as you might expect, sell the Austin Healy and send the money to feed the poor. Instead, he had the Austin Healy sent back to Philadelphia, where it was put up on blocks. Meanwhile, in Boston, he bought a truck and one of his first stops was the local Saks Fifth Avenue, where he bought, not one or two, but a dozen blue cotton chambray shirts, which were then referred to as work shirts. So he had this man-of-the-people disguise that he maintained throughout his college career.

That transparency was perhaps extreme, but I don't think it is significantly different from the prevailing feeling. The proof that this was a costume came in subsequent decades as we all got older, got jobs, raised families, and turned into what is by most measures at least as greedy a generation as any society has ever known.

Vietnam was a defining period, but not as defining as our parents had with World War II, but at the time it seemed just as threatening. There was a great deal more controversy about America's role in Vietnam than there was with the Second World War after Pearl Harbor.

Not surprisingly, the people who were most vocal in their opposition were the people who were the potential cannon fodder. The emotions were sincere. It's hard to fault someone who is on the con, rather than on the pro side of that debate, but I think the emotional component of it is sometimes overlooked. A significant emotional component was fear, and I would not fault anybody for that.

But it would be well if some of us came clean about that. Let me be honest by saying I was afraid. I was not politically involved except as an aghast observer to what was going on. People were scared to death of being drafted.

They might have thought the war was morally wrong, and they may even have been right, but high on their priority list was the fear that they would be the one to be chosen and would wake up overlooking Cam Ranh Bay.

I never came close to being drafted but I knew people who were. People would swap techniques for beating the draft. One favorite was jamming a wallet into your armpits to regulate your pulse rate and hopefully fall outside the government parameters. For some, this was undoubtedly based on principles of pacifism or "unjust war." For others, it may have been less philosophical.

What really affected the educational experience of everyone in school at that time was the upheaval that was an everyday occurrence. I remember the University administration at Harvard was always treated as if it were the prime mover in the global war movement. I have a hunch that in many cases they were the target of the demonstrations only because they were the only people around who would listen.

People would march around the main administration building chanting slogans, some more persuasive than others, but all in a confrontational and hostile tone. Though we have congratulated ourselves in later life for having brought the war to a grinding halt, it's not really clear to me that those demonstrations were what did it. It is my impression that the war ended not when those who opposed it decided it wasn't worth the pain, but when those who favored it did.

The proportions of people committed to Boomer ideals, seriously committed, may be the same that it ever was, but they're not yelling about it anymore, or maybe they're being drowned out by people who are yelling on the floor of the stock exchange. Clearly, if the Boomer generation which is in control of a lot of political, educational, and business institutions today were overwhelmingly committed to those ideals, we might have made a little more headway than we seem to have made.

It doesn't take a majority to establish the stereotype of a generation. I'm commenting on a stereotype, a perception of our generation, and since I don't conform to that stereotype I don't have the virtues associated with the stereotype, and can only hope I don't have all the vices. If my generation helped bring the Vietnam War to an end, I wasn't there to help them.

One lesson we learned from that time is the danger of careless labeling, and any time you're going to begin a sentence with the words the *Baby Boomers*, you're doing exactly that. In the '60s and '70s there were some serious phrases and disagreeable labels hung on people that had a negative impact on social discourse generally. Someone not opposed to the war, per se, could expect to be branded a fascist, and if that person had some inclination to listen to the anti-war message, don't you think he became a little more rigid in his thinking after you called him a fascist? Wasn't he going to be harder to convince?

If you felt the police had acted violently or with excessive force in quelling a disturbance, was the cry of *off the pig* the most effective way to bring the police around to your way of thinking?

If after considerable dialogue you were willing to modify your position and say *don't off the pig,* is that an awful lot better? You still have this polarized society, so polarized that some people responded to the two-finger peace sign by holding up three fingers. The joke was, that meant "Screw Peace!" How could you ever get an opponent to say that? It seems just barely possible.

Thinking about it, I don't come to any profound conclusion. I certainly have no right to say anything particularly bad about my own generation. I think the worst I could say, and it's hardly damning, is that we turned out to be not as special as we thought at 19 we would be.

Some members of the generation probably had some influence on the end of the war—that particular war—but by and large we were like other generations. We were not world-beaters, not leading the march to the New Jerusalem. And today we're coping with the times as all the generations before us have.

Rick Perlstein

Barry Goldwater carried only six states in the 1964 presidential election. It was such an abysmal defeat that many believed it to mark the demise of conservatism. Arthur Schlesinger, Jr. offered the notion that the two-party system was in jeopardy. Four years later, the Great Society was finished, we were still in Vietnam, Bobby Kennedy and Martin Luther King had been assassinated, the country was in turmoil, and Nixon had been elected president. Rick Perlstein, author of *Before The Storm—Batty Goldwater and The Unmaking of the American Consensus,* explains how Goldwater lost, but how the conservatives won, when a convergence of events occurred in the mid-to-late 1960s that broadened the conservative appeal for millions of Americans, significantly changing the culture of the country.

For the generation that ran politics in the first decade and a half after World War II, the war was a living memory. The experience of Fascism, Stalinism, cataclysms in Europe, genocides, were all living memories for them.

Americans agreed about the basic issues and that the remaining problems were mostly technical, so it didn't require a grand debate. Some thought such debates were highly dangerous in that they led people to a commitment to absolutes which could lead ultimately to violence, and the end of our democratic system. But by the middle of the '60s that assumption was in tatters, resulting in the unmaking of the American consensus.

Tom Hayden, the great left activist, talked about consensus and America being the best of all possible worlds; all that was was a glaze over deeply felt anxieties. I'm not sure there really ever was a consensus. There was a great difference of opinion on fundamental issues such as race and the Cold War, the flowering of the civil rights movement and the awful backlash against it, and women beginning to grow restive in their domestic role. Americans had no language to deal with that, had no political pattern in which to express these new feelings.

When the Kennedy assassination occurred, the nation suddenly awoke to find itself far more divided than it had ever known before. The conflicts were always there, but suddenly they rushed to the surface in a way that people weren't prepared to face, and before long the whole situation didn't seem tenable anymore.

You have politicians like Barry Goldwater telling people that extremism in defense of liberty is no vice. You have new-left politicians and new-left activists questioning the very foundations of American society, the society they grew up in that told them anything was possible and everything was going to be alright— feeling that the rug was being pulled out from under them.

The vast majority of Americans who were poor were white. When Lyndon Johnson spoke stirringly of these people doing without the basic amenities of American life, the picture people got was not of an inner-city family, but an Appalachian family, a family in the rural South. The Great Society was a victim of confidence, consensus, and liberalism of the mid-century.

Lyndon Johnson believed without question that government could accomplish anything it set out to do—this supremely political man making political calculations in his sleep. When he established the War on Poverty in the Great Society programs, he never thought to give them the political cover that he would have applied to any other program.

The Great Society wasn't aimed at the great middle class, which tends to be represented as the moral center of American life. Politically, that came back to hurt him. In fact, by 1966, after the off-year election when all these conservatives won, he was never able to give the Great Society anything near the funding that he wanted. In fact, you can argue that there never really was a Great Society because it fell so short of its funding goals.

As soon as Johnson started putting out those first appropriation bills and they began falling short on financial terms, the Great Society began to die. He was a victim of his own soaring rhetoric because when Lyndon Johnson spoke so eloquently about the grandiosity of this program to elevate American well-being at all levels, people assumed it was a huge thing. But it did things only marginally, around the edges, when looking at the numbers and actual programs.

You had a polarization of American society. Some believed

America had to get out of Vietnam to reclaim its honor. Sexual mores were oppressive. Richard Nixon couldn't be trusted and was destroying the country's heart and soul. They believed those things so deeply they couldn't hear those who believed Richard Nixon was saving the country from itself and that winning the Vietnam War was in fact a point of national honor.

Take the example of G. Gordon Liddy on one hand, and Hunter S. Thompson, the gonzo journalist, on the other. Both believed the other was the incarnation of evil and their side was the incarnation of good. When presented with identical facts, they saw things exactly the opposite. They both had a following, both believed almost with religious fervor theirs was the way to redeem the United States.

You see these radically different positions maturing, almost calcifying, ossifying, and that brings a lot of strain to society. Neither side was willing to entertain the good faith and honor of the other side— not a recipe for national peace. This is a watershed moment in American society and culture.

There are articles about kids growing up now and how obedient they are and how they believe in parental authority. The individuals who wrote about Generation X, Howe and Strauss, did a study of what they call the Millennial Kids, and they resemble '50s kids.

I think we're returning to a time in which to make it in politics you have to call yourself a unifier, not a divider. To be taken seriously in the culture you have to denounce extremes on both sides. You see the long historical era that began in 1964 with the Goldwater campaign, the beginnings of the Berkeley movement, and the escalation of the Vietnam War now beginning to wind down. I think we're in a consensus mood again.

The Baby Boomers were growing up in a time when American confidence was boundless and a new national ideology was taking shape. It was an easy-credit, no-money-down society in which people were told that America was prosperous and safe and people could fulfill their personal destinies, and these kids took it very seriously.

Individual happiness was enshrined as the national creed, and these kids came of age in college and realized there were limits to the amount of freedom and liberty they could achieve. Kids who grew up thinking the world was theirs, that they could accomplish anything, were disappointed when reality impinged and suddenly the world did not look the way their parents promised it would.

They began demanding more and more liberty, more and more freedom, becoming more and more angry when the goals they thought were their birthright ended up impossible to redeem.

The '60s flow naturally from the '50s; a bell-bottom trouser is but a '50s tailfin rendered in cloth. In a way, the growth America was undergoing in the '50s was basically reckless and unimpeded. The '70s was an age where people began realizing that there were limits. But the realization there were limits in the '60s caused a lot of anger and frustration in that generation.

You can't underestimate the socio-economic forces at work as the country moved to the South and West. You had these new prosperous areas in which life was good and there was little to complain about. People were achieving the American dream, but the kids looked ungrateful.

In a sense, it was the Sunbelt Conservatives who were the ungrateful ones because they were delivered all that prosperity and well-being thanks to many government actions they were decrying—things like federal housing guarantees, mortgage guarantees, mortgage deductions, and all the industrial development the government poured into the South and West.

You wouldn't have the '60s without the economic boom that preceded it. They're so intimately tied to one another. Studs Terkel's book *Working* showed hippie kids talking about their parents, saying *oh, they're always giving us this bummer about the Depression and the War and how awful it was and how you had to scrimp and save, and it's ridiculous.* They couldn't hear that, it didn't make sense to them. It was a generation that thought itself a post-scarcity generation.

The country was not ready for conservatism in 1964, but what that key cadre of Goldwater aficionados and crusaders did was create the institutional and organizational infrastructure that would lose, but would live on to fight a hundred more battles.

Conservatism was beginning to look attractive, specifically because of cataclysmic events such as the Watts riots and the Berkeley protests and arrests—the two events that also launched Ronald Reagan to the governor's chair in 1966.

Middle class people were beginning to think of society as something that had been made fragile by anarchistic temperament, but now there was this organizational structure in which to build a political force.

Richard Nixon was an important element, even though domestically he wasn't really a conservative; he picked up the most powerful and useful parts of Goldwater's rhetoric on how society had lost its way. How crime in the streets was the king in our neighborhoods. About busing. About over-zealous civil rights crusaders.

That's how you get that large turnaround after the Republican Party is declared dead and buried.

Robert Lipsyte

Lipsyte is a sportswriter for the *New York Times* and one of the best in the business. Having devoted his adult life to sports, he is convinced the athlete has not changed, but rather is a reflection of our culture. Sports is big business, bringing all that entails to the playing field. That is why those entering a stadium today looking to find 1953 are, and always will be, disappointed.

Years ago, when the Pittsburgh Pirates were winning, they called themselves "family." We always hear "we're family" when a team is winning, because at that point it is functioning as a romanticized version of what we think families should be; what for a long time many of us thought everybody else's family but our own was really like.

For these athletes it's a false family, particularly the black, underclass athletes. For those from shattered and dysfunctional families, the idea of being part of something larger, particularly with a manager as a very strong father figure that they never had in their own childhoods growing up, is powerful.

But it only works when the team is winning; never "we are family" and we're in last place; by that time they're squabbling with each other.

One of the things sports has reflected during the past fifty years is the shattering of loyalty between the corporation and the employee. More and more corporation executives no longer think of themselves as IBM or Xerox, but as marketing specialists moving from corporation to corporation, reflected in sports by free agency. In sports this has been brought about by the intractable greed of the owners, who when given a chance to work out a deal to give athletes a little more freedom, did not, and ultimately lost.

Athletes in the '50s and '60s were exploited, locked into teams. They certainly had none of the freedom athletes have today, but they were still pampered babies making much more than their fans. Just as the salary spread has widened enormously between corporation presidents and employees, the financial spread between athletes and their fans has also widened enormously.

With the advent of television, the athlete doesn't need to deal with the pencil press anymore and have his words filtered through someone else's sensibility. Television is willing to pay for interviews, and he has a false sense that on radio and television his words are going out unfiltered, that he is getting a fair shake.

He also doesn't want to be bothered, and he is surrounded more and more by agents, advertising executives, and public relations people and doesn't feel he needs to [spend more time with sportswriters].

Another major occurrence is the racial divide between athletes and the media. The media is overwhelmingly white, and athletes in many sports are overwhelmingly black, and I think there is a great misunderstanding.

The coverage is—I don't want to say "insensitive," because that would almost say that the writers knew what they are doing. I think it is un-sensitive or desensitive. Their own kind of racism is not a choice to be racist, but a result of the way we're brought up and conditioned in this society.

There is a way of looking at a black athlete—not in terms of the black culture that he grew up in, but rather by these 1950 white, Anglo-American mores of amateurism, stiff upper lip and playing for the team, or the country, and what an athlete is supposed to be. Many blacks come out of a far more individualistic culture where to survive you do whatever is necessary.

O.J. Simpson is probably the greatest example of a black athlete who was able to straddle both black and white worlds. Black fans loved O.J. because he had all this black soul and flash. White fans loved him because he was smooth and ingratiating around them. Michael Jordan certainly is another. But there really aren't that many black athletes who move well in white culture, and they are treated reprehensibly by many white sportswriters.

Albert Belle will never make the Hall of Fame, although his stats are pretty good. He's been portrayed as this kind of morose, ungrateful animal. Look at the attack on poor Darryl Strawberry, for Christ's sake. All these white writers were basically writing how Darryl had betrayed them, hadn't lived up to his potential.

When he was 19 years old, they wrote he was going to be the next Joe DiMaggio or Ted Williams. But by 37 he had spun out of control, had very serious colon cancer, probably depression, and certainly had a chemical addiction. I don't know if we can say all of that is Darryl's fault, although when he keeps falling off the wagon it becomes his fault.

There's always been this sense that black athletes making all this money and not treating the press very well are somehow ungrateful, that they should be thankful for this opportunity in society.

Beginning in the '20s and '30s, Carlisle and Notre Dame and a lot of other schools began this corruption of higher education, bankrupting their souls through major sports programs. How does Indiana—a fine university—justify for so many years having an uneducator like Bob Knight as its most prominent teacher?

In terms of basketball and football, the American college systems are the minor leagues for the pros. Anyone who has gone to a major college knows many of these top athletes are either not going to classes, not headed toward a degree, or if they are, are being carefully moved along into friendly classes, with tutors writing their papers. They might get their degrees, but they're not getting the same education the other students are.

And this is not their fault. They have a full-time job with thirty to forty hours a week of practice and are away from class for days at a time. The idea you could do the same work as a serious college student is absurd. The fact they do anything at all is amazing.

Sports has changed over the past fifty years and is no longer a crucible of character that was sold to us pre-World War II, or even after the war. Learn to play together, be strong, to sacrifice, to dedicate and prepare yourself for war or for corporate life, for being a strong, steady pillar of the community.

We've seen sports slip further and further into being entertainment. And as entertainment, the rules are the same as they are for Hollywood actors or Rock 'n' Roll stars: they can do whatever they can get away with. At the same time, we can think of them as characters to be replaced by somebody a little younger, faster, more attractive, and hopefully nicer to us.

The athlete basically has not changed. Besides all the skill, drive, and focus, it takes an enormous amount of passion. These people really like what they're doing. They love to be athletes. They love their games. Maybe fifty or sixty years ago they would have done it for free. They can't possibly do it for free now because in this culture you would be considered some sort of fool or freak.

Athletes tend to be more reflective of the culture, then change and form the culture. The enormous diversity among athletes has changed the character of sports just as immigration has changed much of the character of American cities. You have Hispanic athletes, and in calling them Hispanics, you're lumping them unfairly. There's a big difference between Dominicans, Panamanians, and Cubans, etc. You've got Caribbean blacks, you've got American blacks, and something we really haven't seen until recently, you have underclass blacks.

Sports has become fragmented and multi-cultural, and it's as vulcanizing and enriching as is the mainstream culture.

Marvin Miller

When Marvin Miller, as executive director of the Major League
Baseball Players Association, challenged baseball's time-honored
reserve clause in the mid-'70s and won, he forever changed professional sports. Until that time, the reserve clause bound a player
to his team in perpetuity; this now ended. Now players operate
under free agency and make their own deals with other teams,
which has resulted in a tremendous financial benefit not only for
baseball players but all professional players, changing the face of
professional sports.

I see no evidence that the typical baseball fan resents the income
of the owner of the team or resents the relatively high income of
entertainers in other fields, whether they be actors, singers, or
motion picture stars. But fans resent the big money ballplayers make.

The typical fan is more likely to think of himself as having been a
potential ballplayer than of being a potential rock star, motion picture
actor, or singer. Therefore, the resentment is greater. He doesn't consider himself in the same category as a baseball club owner, or top
executive in a major firm, where the earnings are much higher than
ballplayers.

When we talk about attitudes toward baseball players, the fans'
only source of information is the media. It's the newspaper writers,
magazine writers, radio and television announcers, unlike many
other fields where a member of the public has multiple sources of
information. A fan's attitude toward players—whether it's his salary
or anything else—comes straight from the sportswriter or announc-
er. It doesn't come from literature, or anything he studied, or firsthand experience. It comes only from the media.

Let me go back before the players organized, to the days of Joe
DiMaggio when there wasn't any union. I mention DiMaggio because
it's an extreme example. DiMaggio had put back to back two of the
most improbable years you ever saw, then became a holdout. In those

days, if you didn't agree with the owner about the salary he was going
to pay you for the following year, you became a holdout. An ineffec-
tual holdout, but a holdout. You didn't sign. I believe he was asking
for $40,000.

He held out until about opening day. Like most holdouts, he
couldn't win against a determined owner and he came back badly
whipped, and his first time up at Yankee Stadium he was booed
unmercifully.

That reflected what the newspaper writers and announcers had
been feeding the public by way of Jacob Ruppert, the owner of the
Yankees. The fans hadn't the slightest sympathy for one of the greatest ballplayers of all time. They thought he was an ingrate.

There are numerous fans who regardless of the propaganda,
regardless of the media, sympathize with players. Recently I looked at
some old mail I received during the fifty-day strike in 1981. It is striking how bimodal the mail was. Letters by and large from fans, some
of it the most vitriolic, hate-filled, disgusting material you ever saw.
But others, most encouraging, warm and understanding.

What I remember most about the period leading up to the end of
the reserve clause was the Curt Flood lawsuit. The great, great
courage and integrity of Curt Flood—it was an experience you don't
often have. The case educated people about the reserve clause and
its inequities. It was interesting to watch views change. Not rapidly,
but slowly.

That lawsuit, which we lost, and expected to lose, nevertheless was
a turning point in the understanding of players, fans, writers, the
public, and even some of the owners. It was remarkable to watch it
unfold. I often think about it.

In Babe Ruth's prime, the owners of the Yankees understood that
paying a man $80,000 a year for playing baseball was catnip to the
fans. They wanted to see who was worth that kind of money. The
Yankees would publicize his salary by holding a press conference
when he signed his contract. They understood the publicity value,
whereas later the owners would run down the players: the players had
become greedy, the players were this, the players were that, the players were getting all this money for playing a game.

They were running down their own product, something the owners did not do in Babe Ruth's day.

I have a very pleasant feeling about it all. There's a sense of accomplishment, and not just personal accomplishment. I rush to emphasize that the major league players during the time I was there were among the fastest learners I have ever encountered. They started out with abysmal ignorance of the economics of the game, and how they fit into it, and ended up knowing much more than the owners.

They were the backbone of the union and still are. I trust that the present generation of players will apply their understanding of where they fit in the coming struggle, 'cause there's going to be another struggle without any question.

PART III

Metamorphosis

Richard Shickel

Schickel began writing movie reviews for *Life* in 1965, then moved over to *Time* in 1972. He still works for *Time,* but for the last fifteen years has devoted most of his time to producing documentaries on the movies. As the country's most respected movie critic, he believes the film *Bonnie and Clyde* was a cultural turning point, and that one of the Baby Boomers' favorites, *Easy Rider*, is unwatchable.

The movies of the 1930s, and the first half of the 1940s, were an utterly dominant cultural machine. Something like fifty million people went to the movies each week. There was a certain amount of competition from radio, but radio was just radio, appealing to only one sense—aural.

Today there is a lot of nostalgia for the old movie studio system. Everybody was under contract—the actors, the writers, the directors, even the cameramen. They could produce what they wanted to produce, when they wanted to produce it. They weren't under the financial pressure a studio is today.

In fact, until 1948, many of the studios owned their own theatre chains and they could pretty much impose content on the country. In a funny way, they did a pretty good job of it. There was a good balance between melodrama and comedy, musicals and westerns. You name the genre and they were providing what we needed of that genre.

They had their best years in the first year or two after World War II and were very prosperous. They couldn't see any clouds on the horizon. Oddly enough, by 1948, when the number of television sets in the country reached a kind of critical mass, movies in the old sense of the word were over. They clung to the studio system through the 1950s, though it was diminishing, and they were dumping their contracts as fast as they could.

There was a powerful sense in the '50s that they had to find some way to compete with the free image machine that sat in everybody's living room. One of the things they tried was Cinemascope and wide screen, which was a disaster in terms of content. The movies became slow and stupid, sort of fraudulently epic, and were not terribly successful once the novelty wore off, and the novelty wore off pretty fast.

Cinemascope was the big hope, and 3-D was a gimmick that didn't particularly work. But it became almost automatic that most movies were made in some form of wide-screen process: Cinemascope or VistaVision or you name it.

The watershed in American movies was 1968 when the old censorship system was killed by Jack Valenti and a rating system was applied. If you look at the movies of the late '60s and early '70s, you see a good deal of experimentation going on. People pressing the limits of what they could say in the movies.

One of the crucial movies of that era—and it was made slightly before the new rating system—was *Bonnie and Clyde*. That's a watershed movie for America. Arthur Penn and Warren Beatty thought they were making a metaphorical statement about the war in Vietnam.

The famous last sequence with all the firepower applied to these relatively minor criminals was historically true. When Bonnie and Clyde were ambushed, some 1,000 rounds were shot at them. Approximately the same number of rounds were shot in the movie.

The reason it's a persistent force is that death is shown as an absurdity, an accident, and that applies not so much to Bonnie and Clyde but to the people they offed. There was a sense, new to American movies, that you can't blame the social system the way the Dead End Kids did, or you can't blame Prohibition in the way that was shown in the classic gangster films of the '30s. This represented a new way in American movies.

Bonnie and Clyde and the *Godfather* movies that came later are a subversive take on gangster shenanigans. We're encouraged to like these people, to see them as warm, family folk who would sit down to a giant pasta meal shortly before or after offing their opponents.

China Town, with the rape of the land in Southern California, is analogous to the incestuous rape of the Faye Dunaway character in the movie, an analogy that hadn't been done before.

There's a new way of looking at criminal life and it carries on in more recent films such as *Fargo* and *Pulp Fiction*.

The notion that death is an absurdity is an important notion that has gotten into the popular culture, and our best movies now are much more anarchical and self-consciously anarchical than they were back in the studio days.

That doesn't mean we're making more or fewer better movies. The average stays pretty much the same; there are four or five good movies in any given year, a dozen or so that are okay, and the rest are junk. I wouldn't say that this is particularly different from the way it was in 1931, '41, '51, '61, '71, '81, or '91. That average stays pretty consistent and I imagine it's an average that would apply across the board in popular culture.

There's probably five good novels in any given year. Not quite five good plays. Quality is always difficult to achieve in any kind of art or presumptive art form. I don't deal much in golden eras or declines, either. I think it's pretty consistent.

There's always a delay in Hollywood in coming to grips with vast political events. You can argue that the very best World War II movie is *Saving Private Ryan,* and it took some fifty years to be made. Most of the movies about the war, and I just happen to have seen a lot of them lately because I was writing about them, were pretty terrible. They're jingoistic, super-patriotic, and of no lasting interest or consequence.

The Wild Bunch is making a metaphorical statement . . . not unlike the statement being made in *Bonnie and Clyde* regarding the excesses of violence being applied to situations in Third World countries. Sam Peckinpah was not a guy who was making statements particularly, but a violent guy who enjoyed violence. I almost never see a movie that strikes me as too violent. It may strike me as inept, but I'm not particularly attuned to violence in movies. I don't think it has a particularly large effect on people in terms of imitative behavior for example.

Movies can encourage certain kinds of fashions, whether they be in clothing or in music. It's very difficult to prove they cause serious imitations. There are always psychotics around and it becomes convenient and easy for them to say, *I saw some people rob a convenience store in that movie and therefore I robbed a convenience store.* I find that *ex post facto* rationalization of bad behavior.

Violent behavior in society is a complicated issue. I was on a discussion show with some academics; academics are always counting violence. They count hits in movies. They count the number of times the Road Runner dumps a rock on Wiley Coyote. I said, "Until the United States has a sensible gun policy and a sensible drug policy, you cannot put the blame on movies or television."

We have a drug culture and a gun culture and both of them are stupidly managed by the political system. I think you should restrict guns and unrestrict drugs and see what happens, because this isn't working.

One of the great movies of the '50s is *The Invasion of the Body Snatchers*. These pods have taken over people's souls and psyches, they no longer have any individuality and have become mindless conformists. You can certainly say those pods are a metaphor for McCarthyite behavior.

There was *On The Waterfront*. Kazan once told me the attraction is the agony of the Brando character. This desperate need to be loved and to be a decent human being who can be loved. He said there's a powerful and true yearning in Brando to do right in that movie. It's what carries the movie. Nowadays, who cares about gangs on the waterfront, but we do care about that yearning, desperate figure.

I have dozens of favorite movies, some of which I've already named. *China Town* would be one. *Bonnie and Clyde* would be another. *Fargo, Pulp Fiction, On the Waterfront*. I love *From Here to Eternity*. I think it's a wonderful movie. I love *Singing in the Rain*. I think that's a wonderfully innocent, charming, delicious movie.

Almost from the beginning of movies, way back in D. W. Griffith's day, there were people who really felt movies represented a destabilizing force in American life. I have always felt there were substantial class biases in that movies were originally a popular art form in the crudest sense of the word. They were made for immigrants, ill-educated people, and I think there was a fear movies would present dangerous ideas.

Almost 100 years later, a little of that continues to cling to movies. They are not quite a respectable art form, for all the talk about it being a respectable art form, and they are still subject to journalistic and political outrage. I can't tell you how many movies were blamed at the time of the Columbine Massacre. Whenever there is some outburst of bad behavior, society tends to turn to an easy target like the movies or television. I think it's perfect dwaddle.

There is a class bias against movies. Movies are not quite a respectable form of expression for a certain segment of the population. You run into very few politicians who are movie fans and very few people who write editorials for newspapers who are movie fans. I think that there's a certain anti-Semitism prevalent.

Movies began as a Jewish business and it continues to be a business dominated by Jews. There are obviously WASPS who work in the movies and have a certain amount of power, but [they are] perceived by the country as a Jewish enclave, and I think it is thought [they] don't quite have the same values we have—that kind of thing, which I think is also nonsensical and ridiculous.

If you look at the history of the movies, it is mostly a history of people striving to be accepted, which means promoting American values, the way Louis B. Mayer did. His favorite movies were the Andy Hardy movies. What were those but expressions of WASP gentility. I think that's nonsensical too.

Movies I like best are those that transcend and transgress. I really love subversive movies. I love Marty Scorcese's work, Quentin Tarantino's work. I'm much less interested in respectable, colored-within-the-lines kind of movies. They're okay, but they don't entertain me very much.

A movie that shows that violence hurts, and where violence kills people we have come to like in the course of the movie—those are movies that are really making an important statement. A really good example is Clint Eastwood's *The Unforgiven*. That's the point of that movie, isn't it? There's not a huge amount of violence in it, but what there is is extremely riveting and discomforting.

It's not *The Wild Bunch*. It's the opposite of *The Wild Bunch*. In *The Wild Bunch*, hundreds and hundreds of extras catch it in the concluding firefight and we feel badly to see Bill Holden, Ernie Borgnine, and those guys go down, but it is not a movie with the same kind of impersonal intensity that a movie like *The Unforgiven* generates.

Bob Thomas

One of America's premier Hollywood historians, with thirty books to his credit, Thomas was there during Hollywood's Golden Era when dialogue made the movie. Hollywood imposed strict standards on itself via the Production Code in the 1920s, but it began to break down in the late 1950s, segueing to the ratings system in 1968.

It is interesting to note that fifty years ago Otto Preminger directed The Moon Is Blue, where the word "virgin" was spoken, angering and astounding many. Now the country is breathlessly awaiting the next Hannibal Lector effort and wondering if a sorbet will be served between courses.

In the '20s there was a series of scandals in Hollywood dealing with dope and murder. The biggest was the trial of Fatty Arbuckle on rape charges in San Francisco after a wild party. There were two hung juries and he was finally determined "not guilty."

Some of the studios pushed the median to the limit; no sound then, but a degree of nudity and what we would consider rather tame sex. There were threats all over the country to establish censor boards. That would have been almost fatal to the motion picture industry because they would have had to appeal these ratings in every major city. So the studios got together and hired Will Hayes, who was postmaster general under Harding, and he set up the Production Code.

When talkies came in, some of the dialogue got a little raunchy, as well as some of the sex scenes. The Production Code was never too concerned with violence, but they tightened up the Code and it became ridiculous by today's standards, and that was what the studios had to live with until the late 1950s.

There were ridiculous things such as married couples had to sleep in twin beds, not in a double bed. No swear words of any kind could be used. Selznik had to pay $50,000 to the Hayes office to use "damn" in Rhett Butler's closing speech in *Gone With the Wind*.

Crime had to be punished. Adultery was not tolerated. Sex of any kind, by inuendo or otherwise, was prohibited. It is amazing that so many great movies came out of the '30s, '40s, and '50s under those constraints.

Otto Preminger's *The Man With the Golden Arm* with Frank Sinatra showed him using narcotics equipment, and that was a no-no. Preminger had another picture, *The Moon is Blue,* in which he used the word "virgin," and that was a shocker. That had never been heard on the screen before.

Meanwhile, the Italian films were bursting forth with postwar realism, life as it was, including sex and language, and a lot of American directors tried to loosen up the Code. Jack Valenti became president of the Producer's Association in 1966, and by 1968 he put in the Rating System.

The releasing companies pulled back from too much sex and nudity because of the Rating System; their major audience was teenagers and if a movie was rated "R," presumably those under 16 were not allowed. Of course, that was very loosely enforced, but even so, they aimed for PG-13, which meant that it could be seen virtually by all audiences.

The studios are not run by filmmakers anymore. They're run by agents, lawyers, businessmen, and owned by conglomerates, and they, of course, look to the bottom line. If they have a big hit, they're going to have a sequel because you can expect about 80 percent of the original gross. There are fine pictures being made but the field is much smaller because most pictures aim for a huge box office and do not require much quality.

If young, impressionable males are subject to a barrage of super-violent video games, violence in movies and television, it's bound to have an effect on them. I'm no sociologist, but in the Colorado massacre there was evidence of that sort of thing, as well as in other school shootings. Valenti will claim there's no connection.

The old days are long gone. The companies are not aiming for art, they want box office. The ambitious directors would love to get their hands on a hundred-million-dollar budget with all of the sophisticated digital effects that are now available.

The audience isn't going to change, it's still going to be young. You have to blast the middle age and older people out of their homes to get them to a movie. Many of them are shocked by the language they hear in films, and it is terribly excessive, particularly in the gangster movies. I can't imagine people talk like that, even gangsters, but it seems to be certain directors' stock and trade.

Earle Marsh

Marsh's The Complete Directory To Prime Time Network and Cable TV Shows is in its seventh edition and is considered the authoritative source on television programming, a chronicle of American television from 1946 to the present.

The single program which made television a viable industry in the late '40s and early '50s was the "Texaco Star Theatre," which became "The Milton Berle Show." Berle had tried to become a radio comedian but his comedy was so physical that it did not work anywhere near as well on radio as on television.

Much of what he did was a throwback to burlesque and vaudeville. He used to dress in drag. Berle was the only comedian who got away with that until Flip Wilson did his character Geraldine in the '70s.

In the early days of television, you had NBC, CBS, and ABC, which was very non-competitive, and Dumont, which went out of business in the mid-'50s. You saw more public affairs programming on NBC and CBS in the early days. There was room for things that had social and cultural significance because NBC and CBS were making so much money they could afford to carry programming they wouldn't touch today because of its lack of commercial viability.

"Talk of the Town," which became "The Ed Sullivan Show," had an impact culturally. Sullivan used to have popular comedians, popular singers, dance groups, opera, excerpts from Broadway musicals, [and] dramatic readings, and in his own way brought some culture to the American public and managed to keep it going for twenty-three years. That show, which premiered in the summer of '48, didn't go off the air until the summer of '71.

Television news began to bring an immediacy to the American public that they had never seen before. For lack of a better term, [it was] a homogeneous sense of our culture—of what was going on in various parts of the country. They tried to break down the walls of racism.

But the real impact started with Vietnam in the mid-'60s when you saw the daily news coverage of what was going on. And it brought the horror of war to the American public and contributed in many respects to the growing anti-war movement that was permeating college campuses at that time.

When things heated up in '62, '63, '64 in Vietnam, the government said, *we'll get in and mop up and it'll be over,* but it didn't happen. It was frustrating and depressing to an American public who couldn't understand why, with all our superior military might, we could not cope with the Vietnamese communists.

Television revealed the plight of African-Americans that most Americans couldn't believe existed. Many did not understand the problems Southern blacks were having. To a great extent, television news coverage of what was going on embarrassed a lot of people about what their fellow Americans were doing.

"The Smothers Brothers Comedy Hour" ran from '67 to '69, until the CBS censors got so fed up with Tom and Dick's reluctance to provide them with a copy of the tape in time to edit things out before the program aired. The one that managed to get around this, which many people may not really think had a lot of political and social satire, was Rowan and Martin's "Laugh In." That was a big hit.

Dan Rowan and Dick Martin, along with George Schlatter, who was the producer of the show, put it together in such a way they could get around the problems the Smothers Brothers were having. The Smothers Brothers said *we're doing it,* and got in the face of the suits at CBS, who did not like it, and they caused their own downfall because they were stubborn and didn't try to find a way around the problem.

"See It Now," and later "CBS Reports," in the '50s provided a social conscience for television and the American public and were the antecedents of the really classic documentary and investigative news reporting which we see today. They provided a background and a platform to build on over the decades.

There were two threads in the late '60s and early '70s that began to change the way television looked at certain categories of people and in which we began to see them. You had the first two career women who were not homemakers, who were starring in shows that indicated women could be career people in a society in which they weren't dependent on men: "That Girl" with Marlo Thomas in the late '60s on ABC, and "The Mary Tyler Moore Show." They changed the way we looked at women.

In January 1971, "All In The Family" premiered. It was ground-breaking because it was the first sitcom to deal with controversial topics in a comedic sense and made fun of the prejudices and bigotry that most middle class Americans had had for generations. When "All In The Family" premiered, CBS had limited hopes for the show. They thought it was funny but feared the American public wouldn't accept the fact that Archie used racial stereotypes and that he was a jerk.

It did not do well when the first thirteen episodes were run, but took off in the summer of '71. CBS moved it from its Tuesday night time slot to Saturday night at 8, and for five years it was the No. 1 show on television. No other show has had a five-consecutive-year run as the No. 1 show, and it averaged almost a 32 rating and a 50 share for five years on Saturday night, which is unheard of.

It allowed Norman Lear much more leverage in the topics he could cover and how he could cover them than any producer had ever had before when dealing with the network censors. He was able to deal with the rape situation where Edith was assaulted in the home, to deal with Maude and abortion.

It turned everything 180 degrees. Nothing since has had that kind of impact. There were shows that became groundbreaking for other reasons; "Hill Street Blues" was the first of the really gritty police dramas that showed cops as flawed characters. Television in the '50s and '60s, even the '70s—doctors and policemen—except in a few sitcoms—were basically gods. They weren't real people, and eventually in the '80s they started to be real people. They had warts, they had flaws, and a lot of this is due to "All In The Family."

One of the things which contributed to what we see on daytime, the Jerry Springers, the Sally Jessies, the assorted people with the lowest-common-denominator, dysfunctional people talk shows, is that tabloid news shows became popular. "Current Affair" was the first really major success in syndication of that genre, giving television programmers a sense that the audience had become very voyeuristic and was looking to be titillated, causing the migration from a Phil Donohue and an Oprah to a Jerry Springer and a Sally Jessie.

If opera was popular, you would see a lot of opera on television. But it isn't. People enjoy seeing others making fools of themselves or doing things they would never do. It is why you see the tabloid shows.

Howard Rosenberg

Rosenberg has been the television critic for the Los Angeles
Times for twenty-four years and is one of the best in the business.
Everyone is a television critic, but Howard gets paid for it, and he
believes television is not the negative many portray it to be, but
rather a positive contribution to our culture.

Television has broadened the parameters of art in the country and
the world, bringing art into homes that previously had not been
exposed to it. Plays, music, just about any form of art you can imagine. Television has been responsible for the creation of an art form
which, though it may sound mundane, is the sitcom. It's almost like
the Sistine Chapel of the airways; it's an American creation.

The arts have been broadened enormously by television, especially
cable television. Originally, I was very skeptical about cable television.
People were talking about narrowcasting, have things on cable channels that could not be supported on regular network channels, cater
to specific interests.

I thought, *that sounds great on paper,* but you've got the same people
moving over to cable television who worked in network television and
they will have the same narrow perspectives. To some extent that's
true, but I think you have to say cable has really broadened television.

Cable has had an impact on network television. "The Sopranos" is
a very popular show and is violent. Other cable programs have a
much sexier content than over-the-air television. Over-the-air television feels this incredible pressure to emulate what cable is doing, to
push the envelope in terms of violence and sex as far as they can.

Because there are so many more alternatives available today, there
is enormous pressure on regular television to do something to cap-
ture your interest immediately, which frequently is violence or sex.

People talk about the golden age of television, roughly from the late
'40s to late '50s, when television was in its infancy. They had live antholo-
gies, many of them emanating from New York, *and wasn't it great?*

My feeling is that it was golden if you felt there shouldn't be people of color on television. It was golden if you felt women should be depicted only as running vacuum cleaners and baking cookies all day long. It was golden if you liked fifteen-minute newscasts. It was golden if you liked live television in which fiascos happened quite regularly. It wasn't golden. It was new and that made it more appealing.

Television is better today than ever. Not that it isn't mostly inept, but if you look back and compare it to what it was, it's far better—especially television drama.

Television gets a very bad rap. Most of it is utter slop, but you can say the same thing about books. Most books are bad. Most movies are bad. Most music is bad. But we don't hear all the music, we don't see all the movies, we don't read all the books. But people watch an awful lot of television. So they get the impression, at least critics do, that somehow television is worse than the rest of the arts. I don't think that's true at all.

I'm old enough to remember a period when there wasn't television. I can't recall what we did when we only had radio, but I know one thing: we didn't sit around having intellectual discussions. Probably just sat around and vegetated.

In terms of television dumbing down society, I don't know if that's true. Has it changed society? Of course, it has had an enormous impact on society.

I don't believe television is responsible for all our attitudes. We're all the sum of many influences—church, religion, school, peers, family, home, other media—but television has certainly had a very great impact.

It has altered society to a large degree. To some degree in a positive way, to some degree in a negative way. Take the civil rights movement. Exposure of the civil rights movement on television had an enormous impact on the rest of the country and showed us what was happening in the South. In that way it had a very positive impact, as showing the Vietnam War on television had an impact on the country.

Politicians have always played to the media whether in 1800, 1900, or 2002. The difference is the media is more pervasive today. We see newsmakers all the time and they are sophisticated and manipulate the media. The media is manipulated all the time, just as the media manipulates people. It's a symbiosis and is endemic to how we operate.

Television is an instantaneous medium and makes us move at a much faster pace. It's made us a more impatient society, a society that's much less apt to take the time to think about things. The classic case is televised debates between politicians. Presidential debates bring out qualities you don't want in a president, somebody who makes decisions quickly without contemplating them. For example, if somebody is asked a question during the presidential debates, and he or she takes a moment to think about it, he or she is automatically labeled as gray and ponderous and unable to act quickly. That's not the case at all.

I want someone who contemplates issues very thoughtfully, who doesn't make knee-jerk decisions. But presidential debates celebrate just those kinds of knee-jerk answers, quick answers, quick solutions to difficult problems. Television celebrates one-liners.

The technology drives us instead of us driving the technology. There is this capacity to do things instantaneously. We have these 24-hour news channels and if somebody hiccups at 9 a.m., by 9:10 a.m. it's all over the media. It's on television, it's on talk radio, and we move at a much faster pace. We're less likely to wait for answers to our questions. We're more likely to jump to conclusions because we're under this constant pressure of time.

There are other ways the news media has had a negative impact. One is *the big lie*, where the impression is our culture is totally violent. Television news has accentuated violence for so long it's created a feeling some call *a mean world syndrome*, where you feel you're going to be confronted, even attacked, by a mean world. The result is we have become a more insular and more conservative society, less apt to reach out and have contact with others. That's dangerous and twists the way society really is.

Who are the people we usually see on television committing these crimes? Quite frequently they're people of color, creating the impression that those of us who are white have much more to fear from people of color than we do from whites. So much of what we see on television depicts them in a negative light, in a violent light. Not that there isn't violence among blacks and among latinos, [but] there are so few alternative images on television to balance it.

I think it's important for critics not to lobby people to agree with them. That's not important at all. To get people to think about the medium they're watching—that is very important.

Television is a very powerful medium. It's important not to be driven by the technology, but for us to control the technology and channel it in a very positive way so it will benefit society. It sounds very pompous, but it is very important.

Ed Rosenblatt

An owner of Geffen Records, Rosenblatt was one of the top men in the recording business for decades. Popular music changed forever with "Rock Around the Clock" in 1954, but music passes through different phases because it reflects society at that particular time. Music aimed at the 12-to-17 market will always be successful if for no other reason than kids will play it to annoy their parents.

Kids were buying records in 1956, but they were not buying the Four Aces, Kitty Kallen, or Patti Page. They were buying Elvis, and a lot of R&B. In those days they were called race records, or R&B, and became available in stores in white neighborhoods.

In the late '50s and early '60s, the 12-to-24 demographic bought at least 70 percent of the records. For kids coming through the '60s, the music helped them as it related to their involvement in politics, the Vietnam War, civil rights, and gave them in some ways courage and brought people together—gave them a common bond. For those people, music continues. There are artists today who are making records well into their fifties and sixties.

You look back on the Beatles and they look anything but frightening. In the early '60s they scared a lot of middle-class people because of their clothing and particularly the long hair. Long hair somehow scares the establishment. When the Beatles started getting into the drug part of their music and the maharishi, it reflected the times. Those were strange times we went through in the '60s. In many ways we're still feeling it today.

The '60s polarized the country. You're for the Vietnam War or against the Vietnam War. You were for drugs or against drugs. You were for women's rights—against women's rights. You were for civil rights, meaning primarily blacks, or you were against it. You were for abortion or you were against it. You were for sex or you were against it. We're feeling that kind of polarization today, with Congress and

people who grew up during the '60s—Democrats and Republicans—
we cannot find a middle ground.

It is the white, middle-class kids who are giving huge sales numbers
to these rap records, and the parents go nuts. They don't understand
it, don't get it. It's not necessarily rhythm intensive or music intensive.
It is lyric intensive. The kids today just love that. They love to mimic,
both in music and in dress, the urban community.

Popular music is a piece to the cultural puzzle. You have to throw
television and film into that. You have magazines, newspapers; there's
been an incredible loss of innocence. There was an article in the
paper the other day about films of the '30s and '40s; the screwball
comedies, the very rich guy and the woman—they never talk about
sex but it's always there, and there's always the fadeout at the end
when they kiss.

Today you see things on television you did not see in the movies in
the '30s, '40s, and '50s. The biggest thing is the loss of innocence,
because kids today are talking about sexual acts like it was nothing,
stuff we didn't know about until we were 25 or 30 years old.

I grew up in an innocent time, an easier time to grow up. Kids
today have a lot more to worry about. I graduated high school in the
early '50s in Queens County in New York, and there was talk about
marijuana at a high school twenty miles away. But it was never in my
area. Today it's in every school, whether private or public.

Music is always evolving and we've gone through a period the last
three years where in addition to rap music, the bigger selling records
have been these young male bands and young female solo performers. Rock music has been quiet, but it will get more rock intensive.
Then rap will die down and something else will emerge.

Michael Jackson

Jackson began his career in talk radio at KEWB, Oakland, California, in 1961 before it was called talk radio. Contrary to most of the genre, Michael is civil and polite, respectful of the opinions of his callers. He has always involved himself with the most controversial issues and stands his ground. He is living proof that you can be soft-spoken and still be bright and effective.

I had been a disc jockey at KYA in San Francisco and then went to KEWB in Oakland to do the same shift—midnight to 6 a.m.—and they said do whatever you want. I played one record my entire year and a half there—Elvis Presley singing "Blue Suede Shoes"—and became a talk show host.

After playing the record, I said, "Isn't it wonderful to live in a democracy where a simple soul like Elvis Presley can earn as much money as the entire faculty of the University of California?" And that brought threats. I put them on the air and thus began a year and a half that I knew would do one of two things: make me or break me.

I ripped and read my own news, answered my own phones, and talked for six hours. In those days most talk show hosts would simply burp the listener, thank them for the call, and make nice. I decided to talk about the things the kids at Berkeley and emerging flower-power children in San Francisco wanted to talk about. *Time* discovered me, called me the All Night Psychiatrist, and that got me known at the Hungry I, which was the "in" place then and politicians began to line up to come on the show. We were, I think, the first hospitable controversial talk show. I was open to all points of view, and still am, and showed respect for others. After the *Time* article, I received offers from L.A.

I left and began at KHJ in L.A. in the days of hootenannies and also did a late night show. I had an eight-minute break at midnight in which to get over to the TV studio, put on make-up, and go on camera. It was four hours on radio, followed by half an hour on television.

When KHJ changed to all rock, I moved over to KNX and lost my job for being controversial regarding an issue that I thought was historic and significant—the Watts riots in 1965. Management said *shut up, enough already, nobody cares.* I kept saying it was history in the making and came off the air one night and there was a sign on the door signed by Bob Sutton, the general manager: "Michael Jackson is not to be permitted back in this building again."

I had an agent that didn't do his job, and I would call him and ask why they did not want me. And he never had a sufficient answer. And after eight months, I decided to give up radio because nobody wanted me. My wife said before you do, call the station you would most like to be with. So I called KABC, and Ben Hooverman said, "Where the hell have you been? I've been looking for you."

Two weeks later I was on the air at KABC, and I spent thirty-two years there and was in syndication for ten years.

Talk radio is driven by program directors who in the main come up through sales, not through the news department nor through talk radio backgrounds. Their theory is . . . be in their face . . . be strident . . . use the caller to your advantage . . . don't ever believe the forum is public opinion . . . bounce your opinion off them.

That succeeds for many, but not for me, because I can't do it. I wasn't trained that way, and I don't like it. I don't find it to be what talk radio should be—showing hospitality. I don't find it to be enlightening, informing, and entertaining.

Talk radio is evolving and changing now. Nobody will be as good as Rush Limbaugh at being Rush Limbaugh. But look what's happened to him? He's become the mouthpiece of the administration. He was unique when he was strident and anti-Clinton. Now he's an apologist for George Bush.

Most who take that approach are Johnny-One-Notes. As if the whole nation is only concerned about politics and the whole of talk radio is to stir the fires of disrespect between conservatives and liberals. Most people don't give a darn about that. They care about the things that are close to them. That's why I speak about everything, or try to.

Talk radio made a cottage industry out of attacking Bill Clinton, trying to tear him down, and he did a pretty good job of helping them. It was understandable that there was an adversarial relationship between Clinton and most talk show hosts. He usually returned my calls. I placed them judiciously, and Hillary was the same way.

I was appalled by Clinton. My comment on the air was if only he'd married Lorena Bobbitt he would have been great. Fortunately, though, he married a woman that I happen to be a true fan of, not a sycophant, but a fan of what she's become, how she's endured and survived. I think that he was, and still is, the most magnetic of personalities.

We wished that he was more on the straight and narrow, that he was more monogamous, faithful. But if we have any level of knowledge at all, we remember Ike played around, JFK with anything he could, LBJ as well. I think it's understandable Nixon didn't.

We're living in times when everybody and anything is fair game and Americans can accept almost anything except lies, which is strange. We are big enough to be able to accept any shock, but don't lie to us about it. [Gary] Condit didn't learn that lesson.

When I was at KNX, management would judge the success of the radio show by the number of busy calls. They had a meter that [counted] the busy calls. Strange, because when I had my lowest rating I had the most calls.

I remember when Abba Eban, the Israeli ambassador, was with me, and my assistant said, "Michael, there are no calls."

The diplomat heard that and said, "No calls?"

This was during the commercial break. I said, "No, Ambassador, would you like every phone to ring?"

And he said yes.

I said, "Then say [a banned word] on the air."

The number of calls is not a measurement of the success of a subject or a program. It's how the time is filled.

People don't need to call if you've got a worthwhile audience, a substantial audience. They don't need to be heard. They just want to hear what's going on. Are the people who listen to the program well informed? I think each of us gets the audience we deserve, so if a show has dumb calls, the dumb host attracted them. That includes me. But if you get bright ones, I think you're entitled to say you attracted them as well.

It is frightening we have reached a stage where newspaper readership is down, but tabloid readership is up. I think it is frightening that we have reached a stage where 12 percent of the American public gets their news from David Letterman and Jay Leno. But at the same time, there never has been more news available, to more of us, all the time.

From the cable networks to the internet. From newspapers to the regular television channels. From talk radio to all-news radio. I think we are factoid-filled. But with all the money the networks put into their coverage, with all the camera crews they send all over the world, the local news, with the car chase, will get a higher rating.

Americans communicate better than any other people in the English-speaking world. It doesn't matter whether they come from high estate or low, no education or the highest quality university, big city or small, urban or rural. When Americans speak, we understand what they mean.

Americans do something the Brits have never learned to do. In England the language separates people. In this country it doesn't. In this country you'd swear the people were born with a microphone in their mouths. Have you ever heard anybody sound nervous on radio? Try it in Britain. People sound so affected, so uptight—not everybody, but a large percentage are nervous. Americans are at home talking.

I would go back to something we were discussing before, the conservative talk show hosts. They love to brag that they're making a massive impact on public opinion. Maybe they are, but it's a negative influence because since they have gained in popularity fewer Americans are voting. So if they're that influential, it has to be a negative influence because fewer are voting.

When you have situations like Florida and the outcome of the last election, when you hear about votes not being tallied, when talk show hosts criticize politicians and programs to the extent they feed off it, I think it's turning us into a bunch of cynics who don't want to vote.

I've been most successful letting my audience know that being a liberal is worthwhile. My biggest failing is not letting enough of them know that being a liberal is something worthwhile. It isn't a dirty word and I think I've succeeded to some extent. Because there are more conservative talk radio hosts than liberal, I've obviously failed in some respects.

My first stop in this country was small-town America and I fell in love with it—Springfield, Massachusetts. There's something about big-city America that isn't that much different from small-town America. It's a truly amazing nation with the differences in topography, climate, altitude, linguistic and educational skills, the different heritages of races.

Where else in the world will you find anything like this? That's what makes America the most perfect audience for talk radio. And if I had to narrow it down still further, I would say Los Angeles is absolutely Number One, where the stone hits the water, causing a ripple effect on just about every issue of the day.

We're the place where so many new ideas are spawned, not always good ones, but it happens here. We are polyglot. We are an amazing nation.

David E. Smith, M.D.

Dr. Smith, founder and president of the Haight Ashbury Free Clinics, Inc., has been fighting drug and alcohol abuse for over forty years. He contends we are losing the battle, but that treatment and rehabilitation programs can be very successful. The problem is that most addicts do not enter rehabilitation programs. He is one of the leading medical authorities in the country on drug and alcohol abuse, and believes nearly every family is affected by the problem.

I'm a physician with a specialty in addiction medicine and clinical toxicology. I started as a medical student at the University of California at San Francisco Medical School in 1960. The Medical School bordered the Haight Ashbury so I lived there. I also attended graduate school in pharmacology and took a special interest in psycho-pharmacology, which is the study of the effect of drugs on the mind.

Following my internship, I took a two-year post-doctoral fellowship in clinical toxicology, which is the study of diseases produced by drugs, and again lived in the Haight Ashbury.

I was doing research with psychedelic drugs including LSD, sticking LSD in white mice. I would walk home at night and see the beginning of the psychedelic counter-culture and all the music, anti-war, and civil rights groups. I also saw the medical system was not responding to the drug problems that the kids had, so I started the Haight Ashbury Free Clinic as a response to this youth crisis during the Summer of Love in June 1967. Our clinic was founded on the philosophy that health care is a right, not a privilege, which was a very radical statement in the '60s.

San Francisco at that time was a center of political and cultural activity, the political activity in Berkeley and the counter-culture activity in San Francisco. In fact, The Mississippi Freedom Riders organized in San Francisco.

I came up with the founding principle of our clinic that addiction is a disease and the addict has a right to treatment. "Free" was a philosophical concept, not just that we didn't charge at the point of delivery of care. I mention that because that's one of the big cultural changes that has occurred. President Clinton in the '90s used our slogan, that health care should be a right, not a privilege. That was the basis of the health care reform initiative.

The radical slogans of the '60s have become mainstream issues. For example, 25 percent of the population of the state of California have no health insurance, and our clinic responds to the needs of the uninsured. Since we started our Haight Ashbury Free Clinic in the '60s, there are now over 400 free clinics nationwide.

Another cultural change has been the evolution of the free clinic movement and the specialty of addiction medicine, which is now recognized by the AMA. Addiction is accepted as a disease requiring treatment. Another culture change is Proposition 36 passed in the state of California in which the citizens voted for conversion to treatment out of the criminal justice system. There are many cultural changes that came out of the '60s.

The drug scene became very bad. It saw the advent of speed. Our clinic coined the phrase *Speed Kills* in 1968 as we saw drugs become a lot harder and a dream became a nightmare. And then we saw the increase in heroin. Our clinic started getting federal funding in the early '70s in part because the Vietnam vets were coming back strung out on heroin.

Clearly, drug policy is strongly influenced by the perception of who is the addict. That was when we started seeing not just the counterculture in the Haight Ashbury, but the drug problem becoming very widespread throughout society.

Proposition 36 said addiction is a disease and should be treated as such. Every law enforcement official in the state and the country with the exception of the city of San Francisco was opposed to it. And yet it passed because families were tired of the D.A. kicking down their doors and throwing their kids in jail and using the law that was intended basically for big Colombian drug dealers to abridge the civil rights of individual citizens.

A kid had his car seized for possession of two hits of Ecstacy. Another person had his family farm seized for possession of marijuana. The war on drugs has been a miserable failure. People are demanding a shift in policy and looking for a different approach.

All the epidemiologists say that the current drug revolution start-ed in the '60s. We've had drug problems for a long time, but the cur-rent revolution that moved into the middle and upper class and cre-ated all the trouble began in the '60s.

We do a lot of work with families. Our clinics at the present time have twenty-two different sites throughout the Bay Area and we have about 50,000 client visits a year. We serve as a site for fifty group meet-ings per week throughout the Bay Area, and my wife and I have a small private practice where we deal with addicted health profes-sionals and their families.

We work closely with the Betty Ford Center, and that is where the addiction has hit the middle and upper class. When you're a drunk on Haight Street, and you pass out, you pass out in front of every-body. When you're a drunk in Pacific Heights and you're a wealthy matron and you pass out, you pass out on the floor of your mansion and people don't see it.

We're finding that alcohol and drugs are throughout our society and impact families of every socio-economic class. This is why Betty Ford has been such a powerful force. People holler, "It's not my prob-lem, not in my neighborhood, throw them all in jail," until it hits their family. Then they start seeking help and treatment.

The drug problem has never been worse. Because of the breakdown in the U.S.S.R. there's a flood of drugs coming in from Central Europe, inter-related with the situation in Afghanistan with heroin coming in. When I would go back to the White House to consult with Barry McCaffrey, who was the drug czar, he would show us a flow chart of all the drug trafficking patterns coming in from Afghanistan and up from Mexico. There's a tidal wave of drugs coming into the United States.

There's an accelerated law enforcement effort, but even law enforcement officials say that unless you reduce demand, supply reduction alone won't do it. That's why the shift is toward treatment. And there are major advancements in treatment. Treatment works. It saves money and it reduces crime. If you remember the movie *Traffic,* Michael Douglas at the end said, "What about treatment?" There was nobody there from treatment.

Treatment means in the medical system early intervention, man-agement of the overdose, detoxification, rehabilitation, education of the family, and intervention. Treatment is very broad-based.

There's been more learned about brain chemistry in the last twenty-five years as it relates to addiction than in the whole history of science prior to that. We have made huge advances in neuro-biology and neuro-chemistry making treatment much more effective, but if it was like any other disease, diabetes or cancer, there'd be a massive increase in treatment capacity and funding. Yet you see a decline in support for treatment and an increased emphasis on law enforcement, except in states like California, [which has] said enough is enough.

We need a balanced approach of supply reduction and demand reduction through education, treatment, and to get all families and communities involved. The battle plan as set by Barry McCaffrey is going to be at the community level, with the support of effective national and international policy. It can't be somebody else's fight.

Regarding recovery, it depends on the socio-economic status and how deeply involved people are. For example, at the upper level with the addicted doctors, you get about an 80 percent success rate. As you move down the drug culture the success rate runs like 30 percent to 40 percent. In general, these success rates are comparable to various stages of cancer and diabetes.

People say that's not a very good success rate. The problem is there are fewer people in treatment, so you have to look at the treated population versus the untreated population. The problem is that most addicts don't get into treatment. But once we get them into treatment, if the proper treatment is available, there is substantial improvement and success.

Addiction treatment is the most cost-effective of any chronic disease. You get a much better cost offset for the treatment of addiction than you do for cancer or diabetes. There was a study done here and every dollar in treatment saved seven dollars in health and social costs.

Keith Anderson

Anderson did what few have done: he graduated from Northwestern University, then returned to his high school and taught chemistry, from 1957 to 1993. The most difficult thing for him during those turbulent years was not drugs, racial incidents, violence, or non-performing students, but rather the parents of the students.

In the early '50s, Evanston, Illinois, was a conservative community. The high school was a mix of about 10 percent black and 90 percent white, and that figure held for many decades prior to the '50s. Things were pretty stable.

My dad taught chemistry at the high school beginning in 1928, and even as a young kid I had very strong feelings about the place. My dad was proud of it. He had good students, enjoyed his work, and taught me loyalty to the school, to the community, and to the nation. He taught me to judge people by how they treat you, not by their skin color or religion.

Although the high school was integrated, there was little flow between black and whites. The sports teams did the most to integrate and we got to know each other there. Outside of that, we didn't have too much connection with each other. But there weren't too many problems.

My dad and I were together there for five years. He taught the college-bound students and didn't know what a discipline problem was. He never had one. When I came in I had to teach all levels. And of course we had ability grouping, which eventually leads to some problems, and I had some of the lower-ability groups. Sometimes at lunch we'd sit and talk about things, and [Dad] was totally unaware of how some of the students behaved and their lack of effort. He was living in an ivory tower within the school, and I'm down there teaching the different ability groupings.

The civil rights movement and Vietnam were tied together and there was a lot of pressure from parents then. Groups of parents began to get into the mix with their own ax to grind. Things started to get a little nasty, parents wanting to do this or didn't think this was right.

There was a case when one of the black coaches wanted the varsity basketball coaching job and got the black players to back him. Since the blacks were basically the whole team, they pushed for the black coach. It was nasty. I'd come out of those meetings really upset, one of the few times I got upset about anything in my teaching career.

The black parents had legitimate gripes. The tracking system, ability grouping, it was tough to talk to a class and see all white or mostly white, then walk into another class and it was black—almost a form of segregation. They had some good ideas and the high school addressed the situation and did special things by creating the magnet school with the top kids of all ethnic backgrounds participating.

We had an influx of money when Sputnik went up. They threw a lot of money into science education then and it helped education overall.

What happened in the '70s and '80s was we had "white flight." There were gang shootings. Drugs became a problem. People moved because of what they were hearing and what they perceived was happening at the high school.

The kids I had at the end of my teaching career in 1993 were not that much different from the kids I had at the beginning. The percentages were much better in my classes. I had lots of blacks, had all different races. The kids worked hard. Teachers who taught the very highest-level students were concerned about the strength of the students, but we were winning Westinghouses and still had a strong battery of top-notch students. The education they received was excellent.

The kids for the most part were polite. There was a tendency for some of them to cheat a little, but that happened when I was in high school in the '50s.

I don't think the kids changed all that much, but the outside influences, the music and drugs, certainly got worse.

Kids today have problems because both parents are working. Many times neither parent is home. Kids haven't changed as much as the parents have changed and the effort parents put into it.

One of the biggest problems for schools has been how things have been done—the militant way problems have been approached.

Things could have been done in a more relaxed, effective manner. It has caused a lot of grief.

I think the kids today are great. It's the parents with axes to grind that are fomenting trouble.

The breakdown in the relationship between parent and child is probably the biggest problem we face. The parents you really needed to see were never around. It's not easy being a parent. You will always have problems with your children. The communication sometimes just isn't there.

Stanley E. Engerman

Author of *The Cambridge Economic History of the United States* and
Long Term Factors in American Economic Growth, Engerman is one
of America's most prominent economists. The American economy has grown substantially since 1950, and one of the main reasons is our freedom to pursue a living.

We had a recession in '53-'54 and '57-'58, but they were minor.
During the Eisenhower period, economic policy was good, and it is
always striking that most of the patterns of the U.S. are replicated in
England, France, Germany, and other countries.

Eisenhower didn't get much credit for many things he did. First of
all, there were no major problems. Number two, he was smart
enough to take the advice of a good group of advisors and the economy boomed. Eisenhower had a first-rate group of advisors.

Kennedy campaigned on economic growth and its paramount
importance and introduced policies to promote growth at a more
rapid rate than Eisenhower had. This, plus the missile-gap issue, were
instrumental in the '60 election. Kennedy appointed noted economists who were basically Keynesians.

John Maynard Keynes, a British economist, was a noted and brilliant figure before he became active in politics and argued that government could have a significant effect on long-run economic policy.
He argued that with a combination of taxes and expenditure the
government could bring about full employment and economic
growth and that—and certainly it looked plausible in the
Depression—if you did not have these policies, economies would
stagnate for a long period of time. There'd be no way to generate
growth, [and] population would slow.

The heyday of the Keynesian view was during the Kennedy administration. After the late '60s, the strict Keynesian view began to fade
because of the theoretical attacks by Milton Friedman and others,
partly because when inflation developed it didn't look like this

143

approach could handle the situation. Theoretically, the relative flow of money versus fiscal policy shifted.

Inflation certainly affected what had until that time been a reasonably steady growth pattern during the previous fifteen to twenty years. Again, as we had inflation, so did most of the other developed countries of the world.

Nixon is a bit of a puzzle in terms of policies. While one could understand going off the gold standard, the idea that wage and price controls outside of a major war could be effective seemed a doubtful proposition, a proposition rather unexpected from somebody who tended to be conservative and laissez-faire. It is a puzzle how he convinced himself that wage and price control guidelines could be effective outside of war, and it was politically very difficult to enforce and maintain.

The stagflation of the 1970s has always been one of the major mysteries for economists. People were trying to stop inflation, but things got tighter than they had intended without stopping the inflation. It's always been a puzzle.

The economy turned for the better in the early '80s because people attempted to stop inflation more aggressively. People were willing to believe prices wouldn't rise as rapidly as in the past, that things would become more stable. It was a serious concern for Reagan, and he provided an anti-inflationary policy.

Economies have had cyclical fluctuations for centuries. The cycle has always been there. Reagan looked more in control than Carter and people responded to that.

In England at that time, Mrs. Thatcher came in, and she had a very explicit policy toward the unions and turned things around. There's much about Mrs. Thatcher and Reagan that people didn't like politically, but there were certain aspects which had positive benefits.

Clinton had less to do with the economy than Greenspan. There were indications when he took office that the economy wasn't in that deep a recession, that with a slightly different monetary policy growth might come back more rapidly.

In a sense, the same debate occurred in 1960 when Nixon claimed the Federal Reserve System didn't respond quickly enough, therefore leaving the residue of recession. That was Bush's complaint in '92. Most of the interest from 1992 to 2000 concerned Greenspan and the economy.

Through the Kennedy and Johnson years there was an attempt to implement some sort of Keynesian policy, the focus on using the monetary authority to control the economy. The change has been dramatic. Now most people focus on monetary issues, with some discussion of taxes and expenditures, but not as much as previously.

The government also determines the degree of control and regulation in the economy. It determines the source and control of foreign trade, imports, and exports. In those issues, you get a mixed review in that trade has been loosened in the sense that import tariffs are down, but the government has interfered much more in terms of labor standards, environmental issues, and interfering with trade, which weakens foreign countries.

There has been an incredible decrease in the number of people below the poverty line, the bottom part of the population having higher absolute incomes than they've ever had before. It's a very different world than existed in 1950. The government is making accessible to people certain financial aids [and] health care, which hadn't been done before. If one compares the living conditions of 1950 with those today, it's quite a bit better today.

One of Keynes' great contributions, which he doesn't get credit for since it's not part of his basic economic theories, is that you can control things. That if you watch for signs of trouble, you can avoid trouble. The sense that certain things can't happen again, although in all fairness, in 1929 they had the same type of confidence that nothing could happen. But we have learned quite a bit since then.

Relative to the 1920s, the government's budget is much greater, as it is in Europe as well. The health-care policies, social security, various types of welfare all provide a much broader floor for the population. The extreme poverty of the '30s, even the '20s, is not there anymore.

One remembers forecasts during the war by exceptionally smart people who thought the economy would never be able to recover. Many brilliant economists in the 19th century expected growth to come to a halt because they believed everything had been invented. If you bet against the wise people, bet optimistic, you will be farther ahead.

Over the last forty to fifty years, the U.S. was supposed to be surpassed by Russia, Germany, and Japan. The flexibility in our economy contributes to our success.

I find it interesting in teaching about the very wealthy and the middle wealthy of the degree of flexibility and turnover in the American economy. You don't go from the bottom to the top very often, but there's a lot of churning within the distribution and many of the very wealthy today were once moderately middle class, maybe even worse.

Our freedom of opportunity permits people to make money and often it results in a big payoff.

PART IV

Acceleration

Bill O'Reilly

Fox's "The O'Reilly Factor" is the best interview program on television because Bill O'Reilly is the best interviewer on television.

Following World War II, people came back regimented and molded by the military. The women had waited for them and there was a lot of patriotism. Everybody was feeling good, and they all began to live traditional lives.

There was very little drive in the late '40s and '50s to initiate social change. Times were good, we had won the war, there was no Depression. People were earning enough to have children and buy a home as my parents did. They didn't have a lot left over, but that was all right because they came out of the '30s when nobody had anything. So contentment reigned for about twenty years.

Then in the '60s, as the younger generation moved into early adulthood, the Vietnam situation rattled the country and changed attitudes from traditional to questioning. *Why are we going over there? Why are our people getting ground up? What are we going to accomplish?*

And the government, instead of being paternalistic, became antagonistic. They were no longer looking out for the best interests of the people. They had an agenda that nobody really understood. So a generation within the space of two years, from '69 to '71, turned on the establishment. Boom. With that came acceptance of drugs and sex outside of marriage and all kinds of things that questioned established mores.

But most people snapped back into conformity pretty damn fast. What remained was a much more tolerant society regarding minority rights, privacy, your ability to do what you wanted, the "me" generation—all of that followed from *If I want to take drugs, I'm going to take them. Nobody can tell me I can't. If I want to have sex outside of marriage, fine. If I have a kid, that's fine, too.* There was no stigma. All the stigmas disappeared in two years, and it was a tremendous force in our society.

You had a society that turned around and became more European in its outlook—more tolerant, more diversified, and then civil rights came to the fore, and much more.

There was the good with the bad. There was destabilization of the family unit—bad. But there was improvement in civil rights, tolerance of minorities—good. There was an increased emphasis on the individual—bad. But there were many opportunities created so people like me could advance economically and in other capacities— that's good. You had a whole bunch of parallel stuff, both good and bad, that came with the change.

Now we have a lot of agenda-driven individuals. The best example being people who define themselves as homosexuals—looking at themselves through one activity—sex. They're not defining themselves as Catholics, or Americans, or Greeks, or Irish— they're homosexuals. That's their primary agenda. Their whole life centers around being homosexual.

That's bad. That's ridiculous. That limits individuals and puts them in a position of always being on the defensive. People who define themselves as born-again Christians—the same thing. If that's how you define yourself, you're always on the defensive.

There are many Americans living in those kinds of bubbles, and they're very, very small bubbles. When you get a bunch of them together, they can make a loud noise. And then society caves in to that kind of pressure because a lot of people are cowards and don't want to confront people with selfish agendas. That's not to say you should be pushed around if you're defining yourself narrowly. You shouldn't be. But I think it's a really bad way to look at life.

Politicians realize if they pander to enough groups they can put together a coalition that can get them elected since only 50 percent of the voters show up. If you can attract the unions or certain minority groups or certain right-wing groups, whatever it may be in your district, and they have good numbers, you can win.

That's certainly what's going on. Therefore what happens is the rights and desires of the minority become paramount in our society, not the majority. Now, there's a good thing attached to that because for many years the majority kept the minorities down—the black experience is a perfect example. That was wrong. You can't be oppressing 13 percent of the population because you don't like the color of their skin. That's absurd.

Now, you don't have politicians looking out for the greater good of the country. Primarily they're interested in themselves and selling themselves to a certain constituency. They don't keep an open mind, they're not looking for policies that are going to correct social ills. They're looking to pander and give people other people's money. Ridiculous.

The best example is the federal government will not set up an agency to watch how our money is spent. They don't care. All they care about is making promises, spending money to woo people to vote for them. They don't care if the money is effectively spent, whether it's wasted, whether it's stolen—they don't care. All they want to do is say to a certain group, "I'm going to give you this. Vote for me."

California, Massachusetts, and New York are probably the only states in the Union Hillary Clinton could have won. So she cherry-picked the New York situation. But if she had run in Arkansas, she would have lost. If she had run in Illinois, she would have lost.

The powerful protect each other. Once you get into that *club,* you want to stay in it. You don't want to be a rabble-rouser because you're *in*. The unwritten code is you play the game, we'll help you out.

The best example is Bush got elected because people were fed up with the corruption of the Clinton administration. It wasn't so much they loved George Bush. They wanted to get away from Clinton and those people.

You would think when Bush came in he would have said, "I'm going to set an example and investigate Janet Reno. I'm going to investigate a lot of the things that happened because we know they weren't investigated. I'm going to right some wrongs and set an example that this shouldn't happen in our society and it won't happen again."

Bush didn't do any of that. He basically came in and said we're going to put everything in the past. We don't really care if pardons were sold. We're not going to aggressively pursue anything because I want to bring everybody together. I want to heal.

But for me, those wounds are never going to be healed. The people who resented what the Clintons did are going to [continue to] resent it. It says, *Clinton got away with it so the next guy that comes along may get away with it, too.*

There's no question that once people reach a position of power, 90 percent don't want to rock any boats. They get in, they play the game, they want to keep their power, and the best way to keep it is to not do much. Again, lip service, but don't do much.

Clinton is a guy who basically thought he could get away with pretty much everything and was actually shocked when he got caught, and did only because of the DNA on the dress. But he did get caught.

He understood power. He understood that he had the advantage in any kind of an attack mode. He could go after them and trot out people and confuse everybody and he was genuinely stunned when he got caught and couldn't get out of it, absolutely stunned.

Did he learn a lesson? No. Of course, he continued to do whatever he wanted to do because he's compulsive. People who are open-minded and clear-thinking know what he is, and fanatics don't. Most people unfortunately are looking out for themselves. They're not judgmental anymore. It just doesn't matter to them what this guy does as long as he's playing into what they believe is best for them. And that's the majority of people.

Two things have to happen in our culture. First, the public education system has to be totally overhauled. And that's not going to happen under this administration, that's for sure. Whether somebody else will get elected and do it, I don't know.

Secondly, there's going to have to be a shock. An economic shock will probably be the one that would do it, but America's going to have to get shocked and then realize we're an undisciplined society. We better get disciplined or we're all going to be in trouble. *[Note: This interview was taken just prior to September 11, 2001.]*

The economy is in trouble basically because the Clinton people didn't pay attention the last two years. Greenspan has way too much power, he's not held accountable. They tried to manipulate events and we got killed. A lot of people are suffering. How bad is it going to get? I don't know, but another year of this and that would be the shock 'cause people will get thrown out of work, they're going to lose their houses. Then you'll see an anger rise up and a change in society, but it will take that.

We've been able to speak to working people on television where they didn't have anybody talking to them for twenty years. Television basically skews their broadcasts to the wealthy and powerful. So we've been able to talk to the average person. The folks know we're on their side. We're looking out for them. That's our most important achievement.

The broader issue of corruption and apathy on the part of public officials—I've gotten it across to some people but most people are more interested in what they're doing day to day. They don't get angry about corruption, but the only way things change is when people get teed off, such as the Founding Fathers and colonists did against Britain.

We're getting people's attention. The Buffy the Vampire Slayer crowd, they're not going to come in for news, and you can't make them. Free society has a right to be stupid, so we're not going to get the apathetic, dopey people. They're never going to pay attention and we don't really need to get them.

But the people who have influence in their communities certainly know who we are, watch us, consider our opinion, and that's a first step. We've grown enormously in five years and over the next five years we hope to continue that trend.

William F. Buckley, Jr.

In 1950 the designations conservative and liberal did not have the application in America they do today. People thought in terms of Republican and Democrat, with all that entailed. The shadings and distinctions of conservatism would emerge in the early 1960s, the primary spokesman being William F. Buckley, Jr.

He carried the movement, lending intellect, style, direction, and humor to a cause that had been discredited by Joe McCarthy and the John Birch Society. Buckley has helped not only the conservative movement but also the political process by presenting his views intelligently and with civility.

I think it's pretty persuasive that Clinton liked to take chances, and quite apart from the other temptations of an erotic life, you have the sense that he felt . . . *I'll get away with this*. And, of course, he did.

I think there's reason to suppose that he never leveled with anybody regarding the extent to which he was doing things. My guess is that it was to a certain extent just plain adventuristic, kind of a taunting disrespect of the law. I think that's definitely associated with the whole Clinton phenomenon.

Did the Baby Boomers defend him because he was one of them?

It was in part that, plus the kind of loyalty that tends to spring up in defense of anybody who is the predominant figure of your team. It's rather remarkable there were no cabinet resignations during those critical years '98 and '99. In England some cabinet members would simply resign because they wouldn't want to be associated with this sort of thing. That didn't happen, and this absolutely suggests to me a change in moral moorings.

Clinton was definitely a creature of the '60s and '70s, and as such, his perspectives were permissive. Now, how he will be remembered—

I think it's hard to avoid the conclusion that he's going to be remembered as the guy who screwed Lewinsky, because there is no other feature of his administration that can compete with the prominence that scene had. This is what people are going to think of when they're asked who was Clinton?

A lot will be revealed in the presidential convention of 2004. Clinton either will, or will not, be invited to speak. If he's not invited to speak, that's going to suggest that a certain segment of the American public is unhappy about his role in history, and if that happens, it will be pretty sobering.

For instance, is it likely that Al Gore will come up with some sort of a volume between now and 2004 in which he will simply confess that Clinton did a terrible thing and got away with it and that it has hurt the basic philosophical credentials of the Democratic Party? I hope that would happen. There's a sense that the kind of success that Clinton had sweeps all objections away from him, as was the case, of course, with Napoleon.

We have a far different country now than in 1950 when you wrote God and Man at Yale.

I think it has to do primarily with the loss of religion. But it also has to do with a kind of attitude that economic good times induce. That has coincided with a lack of any avenue for organized behavior. There's no [military] draft. There's no substantial economic hardship, and people tend to feel that gratifications are increasingly important. One has only to look at the figures of illegitimate children, crime, and drugs.

Roger Kimball

Kimball is the author of *The Long March: How the Cultural Revolution of the 1960s Changed America.* He believes the war against terrorism must be prosecuted to the bitter end, that if Americans can stay the course we will win. But he also believes there has been a softening in the country over the past years, posing questions of resolve.

We are in a different war from the wars we've fought in the past. There's no single foe. It's a very diffuse enemy. Victory will not be declared with the fall of a Berlin or a Tokyo.

The gravest danger is if the American people fail to stay the course. Will they be willing to put up with the expenditures, the mobilization, the resoluteness that will be necessary to win this war? I'm not sure it's really sunk in that this is not going to be over in a short period of time.

People who for decades have been used to thinking of the American government and the American military as the enemy were suddenly, when confronted with the events of September 11, put on the defensive. They understood that something terrible had happened. But the response of, for example, Susan Sontag, when she said that these events were really the result of U.S. foreign policies, or the response of a professor at Rutgers University who told her students that if we look for the root cause of these terrorist actions, you have to look at, and this is a quote, *"at the fascism of American foreign policy over the last few decades."*

That kind of response is ingrained in the left of this country, and the left of this country inhabits many of the conspicuous spots in academia and in the media.

There's an ingrained anti-Americanism on the left. Indeed, it might be an occupational hazard of intellectuals that patriotism conflicts with their high opinion of themselves. George Orwell once said,

"There's no idea that you can find that some intellectual won't believe." And that's certainly true.

Ian Forester said he'd rather sell out his country than his best friend. That's a repugnant sentiment, but one you find repeated often on the left, indeed in intellectual circles generally. They're willing to enjoy the fruits of this society, but unwilling to stand up for the institutions that make this society possible.

They're operating with a very faulty view of human nature. They're Rousseauvians to the core, even if unwitty followers of Jean Jacques Rousseau. They believe man is infinitely perfectible and if only there could be more education, more government intervention, we'd be able to transfer the imperfect human material we now have into something glorious.

But human history has shown again and again that utopianism of this sort is not a prescription for a better future, but for misery and tyranny. What you have here is a refusal to accept what the Bible referred to as original sin: that man is a very imperfect creature. That amelioration of social arrangements cannot change human nature. That human societies are very, very complicated, and the best prescription for human happiness is to look at those arrangements in the past that have worked well and to abide by them rather than attempting to change everything wholesale.

That is something left-wingers cannot abide. It's ingrained utopianism that they can't jettison.

One thing that has always surprised me is the resilience of the left in the face of contrary evidence. Look at the left survival on college campuses. They have perfected the art of insulating themselves from empirical reality. Some of the most prominent people teaching in the field of literature and literary theory are self-declared Marxists. They don't get it. It doesn't matter that Marxism has been shown to be intellectually bankrupt and in real social terms a prescription for tyranny and the miseration of any population it's had anything to do with.

That doesn't matter. The facts of the case are never anything they allow to dissuade them from their ideology.

The left intellectually will probably survive and thrive in the university and cultural institutions and the media. I think their chances are probably less good in the world of partisan politics. I think one of the silver linings of these horrible events is it has made people more serious about what matters in life, less susceptible to the siren song of various kinds of utopianism.

It's early and hard to know how this thing is going to play out. One of the things that has disturbed me is the incitement to panic that many of the media outlets have indulged in. They have allowed a desire for market share to lead them down the road of sensationalism at the expense of responsible reporting.

We in the United States have been very fortunate. There's never been a society as rich or as secure or as pampered as we were in the late 20th century and are beginning the 21st century. There's a kind of loss of manliness, you might say, that has affected this country. Fortunately, I don't think it's irretrievable, but it's a problem.

In many ways we have shown ourselves to be completely unserious. For example, putting women in harm's way in the military. It's preposterous. A serious country does not do that. Having women in the military is a fine thing in the quartermaster's office or surgery. They have a huge amount to contribute. You don't put them in the cockpit of an F-14 or in the trenches on the front lines of battle or on a Navy cruiser that's in harm's way.

The feminist movement, among its many baneful influences, has contributed to the feminization of American society where men are afraid to be men. That's one of the ingredients of our current character that needs fresh scrutiny. I'm not saying the women's movement has been all bad. I'm all for equal pay for equal work and that sort of thing. But women should not be afraid to be women, nor men to be men. And that's really what has happened in this society to an extent that is not often recognized as such.

These terrorists are not people who live according to the rule of law. They can't be reasoned with. I suppose you could put them in jail forever, but there are a lot of them. One of the lessons in this scenario as it's unfolding concerns power. America is a very powerful nation, but power is provocative, especially when it's coupled with weakness.

What I mean is although America is very powerful, it has often been called a paper tiger because it was unwilling to use its power. We lacked the moral fiber to exercise power in an authoritative fashion. I don't mean authoritarian. I mean authoritative. In a fashion that is legitimate and just, but also straightforward.

This country has come off a period of very deep self-questioning. We haven't been willing to use our power decisively. Two of our embassies were bombed in Africa and we lob a few cruise missiles somewhere into the sands of Afghanistan, which has the net result of simply irritating the Afghanis and hardening them in their cause against America.

If you're going to respond to the kind of events that occurred on September 11, you have to respond decisively, with great resolution, and be willing to follow through. One has to be willing to prosecute the campaign to the bitter end.

If we persevere, we will win and it will be a great thing for the world because one of the things it will do is underscore the extent to which the democratic institutions of this country and other Western countries like Great Britain really do represent, as Lincoln put it about the United States, the last best hope of earth. These are institutions that promise people not only physical security but prosperity and freedom.

The enemy we're fighting now is not a religious enemy in any normal sense of that word. What it is is a fanatical deformation of religion, and what has to be underscored here is that the Taliban does not represent mainstream Islam. What they represent is a perversion of it. But it's also a perversion that is shared by many other regimes, shared to an extent not widely recognized by important elements in Saudi Arabia and elsewhere.

It's not simply a matter of getting bin Laden and his lieutenants. It's a matter of changing the hearts and minds of millions of people and many regimes in the world.

Michael Barone

This noted historian, author of *Our Country*, believes we have
become a niche society with the freedom to chose our niche, resulting in no universal popular culture. Old-time bounds on behavior
no longer exist, he contends, further complicating matters.

One of the things that's happened to American culture over the
last fifty years is we have moved from a universal culture to a niche
culture—from a popular culture that reached just about everybody—
the movies and radio of the '40s and early '50s. Television broadcast-
ing during the 1950s was aimed at just about everybody, but it also
had a certain amount of highbrow elements to it. "Omnibus" was
part of the 1950s, as was "Ozzie & Harriet."

It was an attempt to package culture in a format that was accessible to a lot of people. The family went to the movies on Saturday
afternoon or gathered around the television set. We were more of a
conformist culture then than we had been earlier in our history, and
more so than we are today.

We were formed that way by the industrial economy that gave us
the entertainment media which reached everybody. We were that way
by the shared experiences of the Depression, especially of World War
II, a war that put millions in uniform. That brought people together
from all over the country and subjected them to the same experiences and privations.

Postwar America experienced a universal popular culture. That
popular culture, in an attempt to be acceptable to everybody, avoided certain things. It avoided increasingly the ethnic stereotypes that
had been part of American popular culture. It avoided prurient matter. Hollywood had the Hayes Office in an attempt to be acceptable
to all ages and groups.

We became once again what I've described as a Tocquevillian society,
which is the normal condition of American society. Decentralized,
individualistic, religious—but in many different ways, including a sort

161

of secular religiosity. We moved from a post-industrial economy where the leadership of big government, big business, big labor didn't run the economy in the way they did mid-century.

We moved toward cultural non-conformism, beginning with the students rioting at Berkeley in 1964 and their *Do not bend, staple, fold or multilate.* These Baby Boomers, unlike their elders, were not happy at being just one cog in a large machine. Of being one person in a large organization. They didn't take pride in it, didn't find satisfaction in it, weren't productive in it.

They did much better. They instinctively sought ways to proclaim their own individuality. Sometimes that individuality was just an assumed membership in some counter-cultural group. But the point is you had a choice. Some of that age group went to Woodstock, others lived the college life of Dan Quayle. There were a wide variety of choices then and no one normality prevailed.

The movies after the 1950s were no longer a family medium. They increasingly became a young people's medium. Television moves hesitantly forward. You have more channels, then cable later. You have the proliferation of television sets. Instead of one family television, you have one to each room. Therefore, broadcasters begin narrowcasting, looking for niche audiences. We see this even more in other media. Radio is the first one to do this; in the '50s it becomes a niche medium.

Baby Boomers fought the war in Vietnam. They protested the war in Vietnam. They participated in the counter-culture. They partied at fraternities. They did a lot of different things. The point is they were a generation which tended to adopt different cultural attitudes, and thought that okay.

If you listen to black talk radio, some of the things that are said will surprise you. The old bounds against prurient behavior are out, even during family hours, on the old-line network television entertainment broadcasts. So to speak of a single American culture at this time is futile. We've got so many.

Some are complaining that we don't have universal popular culture anymore. They're also complaining because a lot of the niche medium partake of the adversariness that the American elite, since the 1960s, have expressed toward their country. Also, toward values they perceive as being middle class America.

There is an American cultural tone and attitude toward things generally. You can trace it back to Alexis de Tocqueville and before.

But it's very variegated in its expression now since the popular culture exists in many niche markets and many of us live mostly within our little niche of society and are generally happy with it.

There's still considerable optimism in this country, a flexibility and willingness to change. You are not necessarily part of the niche you're born into. You chose your niche. That is a difference from many traditional societies. You have a choice of your niche, a choice of where to live, and a lot of people are exercising different choices.

G. Gordon Liddy

G. Gordon Liddy was convicted in the Watergate break-in and served time in prison. Upon release he faced a bleak future as a middle-aged ex-convict. But he was determined to succeed, and with hard work he built one of America's most popular talk shows, carried by nearly 200 radio stations.

Many believe the Baby Boomer generation, otherwise called the Vietnam War generation, were all anti-war protesters. They weren't. Many donned the uniform of the armed forces of their country and went to war. They don't get the credit they should for behaving responsibly and patriotically.

Those who get all the attention are like Bill Clinton, and Bill Clinton was, of course, a physical coward. In any event, I don't condemn that entire generation by any means.

I think the reasons for Clinton's popularity are two-fold. First, he is a charismatic rogue, and people who are not particularly thoughtful are attracted to personality types like that. Second, in spite of the fact that he imposed upon the United States the greatest tax burden since the middle of the Second World War, the economy had been ignited by the income tax reduction of Ronald Reagan which ran its course through the Clinton presidency and for which he received credit.

This is the two-fold source of his popularity, bearing in mind there were a lot of people for whom he was definitely not popular. He certainly wasn't popular with me.

I remember the 1930s and the Depression. Those were not good times, and they enormously challenged the American people, and the American people responded very well. Then we were challenged by the Second World War. I don't think it's generally recognized that prior to World War II we made the same mistake we have throughout our history of reducing our armed forces. In fact, we were less powerful than the Netherlands and Portugal.

Because we had the protection of 3,000 miles of ocean on one coast and 6,000 on the other, we had the time to reverse that situation. The people who went into the armed forces were inured to discomfort and were tough. The infantry is called the Queen of Battle for a good reason. No one has ever won a war without occupying the territory of the enemy, and that will be true tomorrow as it was true yesterday.

Having said that, we have extremely serious problems in the armed forces regarding the introduction of women, and the consequent degrading of standards of performance. We used women in the Second World War and they provided very fine services. But we did it the correct way. We had the Women's Auxiliary Army Corps, called the WAC, and the Navy had the WAVES.

They were billeted separately, had separate female non-commissioned and commissioned officers. They were kept totally away from combat, with the exception of the nurses, who performed excellent services, and the mantra, if you will, was *free a man to fight*.

Men were made for fighting, women were not. We have unfortunately gotten the bizarre idea that the armed forces of the United States are bodies for social experimentation and we have degraded their fighting ability.

One man called me on the radio commenting on women in combat and said, "Combat is, because I went through it, 24-hour days in a hole, freezing, soaking wet, with someone trying to kill you 24 hours a day."

Women lack the upper body strength to be able to pull their buddies out of danger. It is absolutely absurd and presents a serious danger.

Over the years, the virtual destruction of the public education system in this country is the dominant concern of my audience. It was in my youth very good. Then along came the teachers' unions and you are now raising a nation of people who cannot speak the language correctly, who require calculators to be able to do simple arithmetic, and know little of their country's history.

I hear an awful lot of lamenting of this fact. I have stated we ought to have a bumper sticker which reads, "If you can read this, thank a teacher. If you can't, thank a teachers' union."

The two areas in which I have been most successful in educating my audience are the difficulties in the armed forces and with the public education system as just stated. I've been least successful in educating people as to what really happened at Watergate, and that is because nobody cares. There's very little interest. It's looked upon like the Spanish-American War.

Today, young people come up to me, look at me, snap their fingers, and say, "I know you. I know you. Miami Vice."

James Bradley

Author of the bestseller *Flags of Our Fathers*, Bradley believes the American spirit will not diminish, that it passes on to each new generation. The Americans who fought at Iwo Jima are no different from the heroes of September 11. His father, John, was one of the celebrated flag raisers on Mount Surabachi on Iwo Jima.

Prior to September 11, I delivered many speeches regarding the valor of the flag raisers and the boys on Iwo Jima. Afterward, during the question and answer period, I would usually get a question along these lines: "Mr. Bradley, regarding the great valor shown by that generation, do you believe it would be there if we had a crisis today?"

The question was always asked in a negative tone.

I always felt they believed American valor and spirit had changed and that we had become soft. I would generally answer (this is prior to September 11): "One of the reasons Hitler and Tojo decided to fight America was because they believed American youth lacked fighting spirit. They thought they were soft."

Pearl Harbor was considered next door. If we don't fight them out there, we're going to have to fight them here and Mom's going to get killed. Many mothers were getting killed all over the world. My father and the other five guys that raised the flag [at Iwo Jima] weren't warriors. They fought because of the size of the challenge.

I would end my talk by saying, "I'm confident if America ever has a challenge where people feel they have to fight or their mom is in danger, we will rise up and this generation will be the next greatest generation."

At the base of the Marine Corps Memorial, it states "Uncommon valor was a common virtue." I couldn't understand what was this uncommon valor that my Dad exhibited at that time. The rest of his life he was just a mild, kind of meek guy. Then I realized I was looking at the wrong end of the equation. The equation is uncommon valor was a common virtue and common virtue won the battle of Iwo Jima.

These were good boys before, during, and after the battle, then came back and rebuilt their communities. Whether September 11 or February 1945 on Iwo Jima, the American spirit has not diminished. The American spirit—common virtue.

I'm talking not about patriotism, but about common virtue. An example is offered by one of the flag raiser's sons who said, "My dad always said raising the flag was as significant as going to the mail box."

When I was ten years old, I was walking down the street with my dad and he pointed to a janitor walking toward us and he said to me, "If you give that guy a smile, it's free, and he'll appreciate it." Common virtue.

We're peaceful people. We were challenged and we are going out and getting it done. I don't think there's a latent, raving patriotic spirit in America. But when mom's threatened, good boys go out and change things so that mom is safe.

Toni Cook

Cook is articulate and precise, with an excellent command of the English language. No doubt this is why the Oakland, California, School Board had her announce that the Board had approved the use of Ebonics in their classrooms. All hell erupted, resulting in their rescinding the order. According to Toni, the media did not understand what the Board was actually advocating.

I don't think the teaching curriculum has caught up to the fact that kids learn differently. The field of education has not learned that one size does not fit all. In Miami, Florida, kids come to school speaking 115 different languages. In Oakland, there's ninety different languages. In L.A., it's more than 100 languages.

How do we structure the program so there is substance and meaning so all children can learn? American education hasn't figured that one out yet.

It used to be if you didn't produce in school you lost your privileges. That ethos is not there anymore. So much has been taken away from the teacher in terms of capacity. A teacher cannot visit the home, cannot spank the child, cannot have prayer in the classroom, all things we took for granted. It's not so much being deeply religious, it's about what the prayer did; it gave teachers a weapon to use to establish a sense of values and ethics.

The teacher can't spank the child . . . [the] only thing she can do is refer him to the office. That's somebody else's headache. And if the office doesn't know what to do, they suspend the kid. Most of the time when you hear of discipline problems you can almost assume that that teacher is having issues with classroom management.

We have found that African-American kids are failing no matter where they live and regardless of family income. It's a complicated issue. I wish it was simple. It stems anywhere from the value of education in the home to the preparation we give our teachers. Whether we have children or not, we don't really value education in the United States.

In other countries, in terms of the social ladder, teachers are at the highest rung. In most states you have to devote the equivalent of graduate-degree time to get a teaching credential. They've got to pay to take the teaching test, and we pay them on average $30,000 as a beginning salary.

Garbage collectors make more money. When you go to the schools that cost $10,000 to $20,000 per year, the teachers are not credentialed. They've got graduate degrees and may be retired executives from industry. My granddaughter's physics teacher is a retired physicist. That school costs $16,500 a year.

I found in California wherever you had a population that was in excess of 35 percent Latino and/or African-American, the test scores were the lowest. I got a chance to talk to parents and said, *"When was the last time you got a call from a teacher saying 'please come so I can explain your child's test scores'? You get the scores in the mail and half the time you don't know what they say."*

The scores are for politicians and real estate [values]. Doesn't mean that they're not needed, but basically all the noise about test scores is really for politicians to say the school system is doing well, or it's not doing well, or because people want to move closer to the good schools.

What about the Ebonics flap?

I was a member of the Oakland Board of Education, elected in Oakland by district. The staff group from the Curriculum and Instruction Department called a group of board members together and presented them with data on performances revealing that both longitudinally and in comparison African-American kids had been declining in performance for the last twenty years.

We admitted there was an issue and had to do something about it. I put together a piece of legislation that mandated the superintendent to create a task force to look at the performance and achievement issues around African-American kids. I didn't make it a board committee because I didn't want to play politics with it. The chief educator at the time was Carolyn Getridge, and she put together a task force—I think they had three or four committees, one of which focused on curriculum and instruction.

They reasoned that the first thing you had to do was bridge the gap so kids became readers, writers, and thinkers of Standard American Competitive English. Oakland had tweaked the state's Standard English Proficiency Program (Ebonics) and said for every elementary school that has 53 percent or more African-American children—Oakland's African-American percentage at the time—that we wanted those teachers to be exposed to the Standard English Proficiency Program so they could bridge the gap from where the youngsters were.

This is how I got in trouble. In the resolutions it says, "Whereas some African-American children speak Pan-African language"—in academia, it's called African-American Vernacular English. Others call it Ebonics, and the press stuck to Ebonics. All hell broke loose.

Our position was that from a cultural perspective the children spoke a language pattern that was not complementary to the marketplace. The marketplace spoke Standard American Competitive English. The teacher training methodology said that we can accomplish the goal because this is the language the child speaks at home. We're not going to make a value judgment of good or bad. The child is going to have problems with the verb "to be," as do the children who speak an Asian language, because it's not in their language pattern.

We want them to be readers, writers, speakers of Standard American Competitive English. Why? Because if they can't speak English, they can't do the rest of the stuff. But they can't read it because it's all written in Standard American Competitive English. That was what the Curriculum Committee focused on, and when the press, (A), focused on Ebonics, they missed it; and, (B), they never focused on the other nine recommendations that came out of the task force.

Teachers didn't have to speak it, just understand what they heard. Nobody ever thought that the Africans who were brought here had a language. They had many different languages, but the law said you couldn't go to school, so there was never any developmental method.

All we wanted to do was be able to understand what it was you *heard* so that when a youngster talked to you, instead of making a value judgment of right or wrong, you understood what was spoken and had a strategy.

It bridged the gap from what the child speaks to where the child must go. The child must read, speak, and think in English.

When they conduct teacher training, the assumption is that the home language is English. Our assumption was that African-American children, the ones that were in our schools, spoke something other than Standard American Competitive English. Linguists label this language African-American Vernacular English, Pan-African language, or Ebonics.

The resolution passed unanimously. Subsequently the board was accused of passing a piece of legislation in which the teachers were required to now speak Ebonics to the children. And I said, "Maybe we all have problems with English because this is not what this resolution said. I don't know where you guys got that."

The system felt so battered that they removed all of the elements of the Standard English Proficiency Program Training and kids are continuing to perform at or below grade level.

There is no Standard English Proficiency Program Training [Ebonics]. That means the teacher gets no training on how to identify an Ebonics speaker. Therefore they have no strategy on how to correct an Ebonics speaker so they can become readers, writers, speakers of Standard American English.

Latino and African-American kids [make up] about 75-80 percent of the population in American urban areas, and neither are performing. The drop-out rate is high. The attendance rate is low. The kids are not performing, and you are all messing with my Social Security.

Expectations are low, as evidenced by the fact that high schools in deep inner cities have few, if any, honors or advanced placement classes. And most of what they teach is irrelevant.The teachers are scared to talk about current events.

The kids have a good idea about what they want to learn. They're asking for a global education. Teach something about all the kids in the classroom, make a second language mandatory. Why is it that kids that come from other countries get to keep their home language and have to learn English? Kids who come from rural areas, or from African-American homes, are made to feel ashamed of their language and are not taught English.

I was never attacked openly by the English-only folks, and I was glad, because that wasn't our debate. We didn't say "only." It's that the primary language in this country is English, and in order for our kids to excel, they have to have an understanding of that language.

The lower income people understood what we were trying to do. I was not prepared for the outburst from the black middle classes where they were not Ebonic speakers and I said *uh-huh, that's 'cause you've been code switched.*

We're the only people who describe our skin when it is not oily as ashen. That's an Ebonics term. Ebonics means black language, black ebony language. The two words put together is Ebonics.

In African-American Vernacular English, from the linguistic point of view, they have traced the language pattern back to certain African countries to get some idea of the language of their ancestors. Everybody they brought here spoke a language other than English. If you had no formal training on how to bridge the gap, and it was against the law to read even the Bible, our ancestors started out not understanding the English pattern. So when they tried to fit the English word on top of the word that they knew, it came out kind of crazy.

Howard Fineman

Along with being the chief political correspondent for the Washington Bureau of *Newsweek*, Fineman is one of the most knowledgeable commentators on television. He believes we have entered the age of technology and that the world will never be the same again. The challenge, since our technology is out in front of the populace, is to master it for our benefit and advantage.

Technology is one of the drivers of social and cultural change. We view the world, the universe, ourselves, and society completely differently because of technological change. The concept of distance has been obliterated. The concept of time has been made more malleable. The concept of leadership has been changed by technological progress.

Television is obviously crucial, one of the enormous facts in our lives. If I'm not mistaken, the number of hours the average American watches television has continued to creep upward and now exceeds eight hours a day. If people are awake sixteen hours a day, and if this number is to be believed, then the average American spends half his waking hours watching television.

Our notion of reality has been altered. The distinction between real life and virtual life has become fuzzy and people shift back and forth between the two at will, with increasing confusion about which is which.

Technology has expanded our view of the universe. Space exploration helped define the last half of the 20th century. We see an infinitude we didn't know before and see ourselves traveling in it in a way we didn't see before. That has opened up huge new frontiers, and we're only beginning to explore the implications. I used to think the movie *2001* was sophomoric, but, of course, I thought that because I saw it when I was a sophomore.

We are expanding our view of the universe and beginning to move

177

out into the universe. We're also moving deeper into our own genetic history, into our own biological history.

We are learning to manipulate it so it's changing the concept of destiny, the concept of free will, the concept of what we can do with, and to, our own bodies, not just as individuals, but as a human race. That is hugely profound and takes the whole idea of free will to a new level that we are going to have to deal with theologically and politically.

Technology is well ahead of our ability to deal with the questions that it raises at this point. I think a big part of the next half century is to come to terms as a global society, as a human race, and as a country, with all of the implications of the questions raised by these things, the revolutions in ones and zeros, in the binary mathematics that has led to the computer revolution, further obliterating time and space. Obliterating the idea of all things being eventually lost because we can now pretty much save everything.

All we need is the disc space, and we're rapidly developing that. Obliterating distance by the speed of communication through modems and optical fibre. Using radio waves for cell phones, the mobility of society, the fact no one can ever be lost, digital revolution has obliterated the idea of privacy. The freedom of women in terms of breaking the connection of sex and reproduction, largely a function of the pill.

Generally speaking, we embrace change; but we can't keep up with it even though we try. For the most part Americans are not Luddites. In the Industrial Revolution it was the steam engine that was the multiplier, and the combination of the steam engine and the wool and cotton industries created the huge multiplier effect that led to the growth of the British economy. Digital is the equivalent of that, like the digital steam engine, if you will.

There are too many questions raised about who controls the genetic heritage of man. I think we are going to have another argument over whether the State controls the means of production and distribution. We decided in the end that it did not or should not; that was what communism was about.

We're going to have a similar argument over who controls the genetic means of production and distribution. Is it just individuals? That's what the Catholic Church believes; probably most religions believe that. But where's the government going to be on that?

Where's the free market going to be? Are we going to be able to buy and sell perfect people? These are profound questions.

The cultural side helped lead to the social side. One could argue that it was a combination of television and radio that helped make that possible because we began to see black people that we had not seen before. We saw the water cannons on the Pettis Bridge that we had not seen before. We listened to music that we had not heard before.

That inevitably lead to breakdowns of racial barriers. But the big story on a social level in the second half of the 20th century is the liberation of women. Not entirely based on technology, but still to some extent.

Radio, television, the pill. It's all driven by technological change. The worshiping of youth. You tend to forget that many of the Founding Fathers were young men. The post-World War II baby boom—the legacy of World War II when all the G.I.'s came home— was a worship of youth that didn't exist before. Now the Baby Boomers are visiting the same thing upon their children which is Generation Y, a bigger generation than the Baby Boomers; 80 million compared with 75 million.

Our big challenge diplomatically over the next half century is going to be to deal with our success and not have the rest of the world rise up and try to take it away from us.

Kevin O'Brien

O'Brien has his own radio consulting firm. After twenty-five years in the business, he is appalled by the conduct of many business people. He believes a lot of it can be blamed on the Baby Boomers and their quenchless need to gather, hoard, and amass.

I began in radio in the mid-1970s when the industry was fairly mom-and-pop. FCC rules kept any one company from owning more than fourteen stations. I started out as an air personality, then sportscaster and program director. I didn't deal with financial accountability until I moved into radio sales in 1983.

In the '70s and early '80s, things were pretty straightforward: if a person gave you his or her word, it was a deal. Even living in Las Vegas from 1978 to '82, a town with a questionable reputation, when a person told you something it happened. No questions, no signed contract, your word was good enough.

In the '80s I moved into sales, then management positions in California and Denver. As the decade progressed, business became more avaricious. It was a little less for you, a little more for them, and I began to see an increasing amount of people rationalize a lower standard of behavior to make more money; their word no longer meant as much. I did millions of dollars of business in the '80s and can count on one hand the number of times a signed contract would have been needed to ensure someone kept their commitment.

The '90s brought about an erosion of ethics and standards in our business I never thought possible. I witnessed more and more advertisers negotiate detailed contracts *in good faith,* then walk away without blinking an eye. Most of the offenders were well-known national and regional brands. The '90s taught us to insist on signed contracts and still not be surprised when the other party tried to back out.

The ethical erosion of some radio companies goes hand in hand with greatly relaxed ownership rules, consolidation, the creation of huge, publicly traded radio companies, and the pressure to perform to higher, and sometimes unreasonable, financial expectations. In 1981 a company could own no more than fourteen stations. Now the largest radio company owns and operates over 1,200 stations.

Radio revenue has also grown, from $4 billion in 1981 to nearly $20 billion in 2001. The industry has benefitted greatly from the increased revenue, but many individuals have not, as jobs in almost every department have been reduced to increase efficiency and profitability. The emphasis on squeezing every dollar of cash flow at almost any cost has caused management to throw the long-term stability of their operation out the window. Ethical crimes are being committed every day, rationalized in the name of responsibility to owners and investors.

Many people still do their business honestly and I'm lucky that I get to work with many of them. Yet it's amazing the extent to which some people rationalize behavior that is dishonest or destructive. What's disappointing is that some of the most high-profile and high-profit people in the business have disregarded their employees and the long-term security of their companies the most. Yet they are written about and looked up to because they "get results."

Since some of these people are regarded as business role models, it's become easy and almost fashionable to toss aside what's right for employees in the name of higher profits. Ours has become a business culture of rationalization as much as one of being profitable while doing the right thing.

Wall Street has become the new Golden Rule, the catch-all excuse for doing just about anything, ethical or not, in business. We cannot blame Wall Street as some vague entity, because we are Wall Street. All of us who invest in the stock market and have expected or demanded unreasonable returns on our investment are responsible. Our expectations are being delivered (or not) at the expense of jobs, corporate integrity, and what's left of loyalty between a company and its employees. We are using our investment dollars to further erode the culture we claim to be trying to save. The guy next door who works for the phone company was laid off. *That's a shame, but thank God I got my dividend.*

The folks at the top of the corporate food chain release incredible revenue and profit goals that could only happen if every planet and star in the universe lined up just right, out of fear that the Street will punish them if their promises are too low.

When, as has happened so often, reality can no longer be hidden, these very same people hold splashy calls with the financial community and submit "revised guidance," which is another way of saying, "I was wrong, but now want credit for accurately revising our performance estimates downward." Then, when the lowered numbers are delivered, they expect backslaps and high fives because they *delivered the numbers*.

Don't expect loyalty if you're practicing mercenary hiring. A manager who attempts to build loyalty and goodwill by saying "our employees are our company" in public shows his colors by telling a manager, "You're a hired gun . . . you'll have my support as long as we need your gun." Kind of gives you goose bumps.

So why doesn't everyone avoid the lure of maximizing profits at any cost and simply do the right thing? The problem with doing the right thing is it isn't cutting edge or glamorous or headline-grabbing or quotable. Doing the right thing sometimes means not bringing every dollar possible to the bottom line, and that's a price too many are afraid, or unwilling, to pay.

Many of the changes in business, good and bad, can be laid at the feet of Baby Boomers. Boomers were the first generation that believed success is a birthright. Many Boomers have a sense of entitlement . . . a feeling they deserve things without having to invest the same effort or serve the same apprenticeship their parents did.

Relative to their parents, Boomers are fat and lazy. This is exactly the way Boomers feel about the Gen-Xers behind them. Baby Boomers are great rationalizers: whatever someone wants to do, no matter how wrong, can be rationalized in the name of something else. That mentality is not new (see Holy War in your encyclopedia), but Boomers have perfected it.

Boomers love money. During the dot-com boom, Boomers saw Gen-Xers, and even a few Gen-Y's, making boatloads of money with no structure, rhyme, or reason. Lots of money in younger hands breeds Boomer envy, so Boomer venture capitalists, Boomer investment bankers, and Boomer business people saw a new excitement and couldn't wait to get in on the action.

Hell, Boomers caused the frenzy by throwing stupid sums of money at new companies set up in broom closets staffed by two 15-year-old nerds and a computer. They couldn't stand the thought of missing out! Some Boomers got rich and some held on too long and lost a bundle, but once the bubble burst they all said they knew it was an aberration and that it was ridiculous. Why then did so many hang on as things went into the tank?

For many Boomers wealth is no longer quiet and modest, and when it is acquired primarily through luck and good timing, the newly rich strut and preen as though the money came their way solely as a result of their keen skills and superhuman abilities.

Boomers have become their parents . . . old. And the worst thing Boomers can imagine themselves as, other than dead, is old.

Dr. John G. Stoessinger

Dr. Stoessinger is as bright as they come. He is a leading educator and author of ten books, with a Ph.D. from Harvard, and very little escapes him. He has studied and invested in the stock market for years, fully understanding the risks. But risk is one thing; corporate fraud is another. Like many, he is incensed and wants to see those responsible for illegal corporate acts pay a steep price.

In the '80s we had [Ivan] Boesky and [Michael] Milken, except they were financiers and traders. Now we have the top people in corporations doing unethical things, which is relatively new. People in positions of great responsibility who are supposed to be role models for the business world to commit such acts, if not criminal, are certainly immoral.

When you have a major boom as we did in the Reagan years, some of the rules were no longer observed. That's why you had the Boeskys and the Milkens, because anything went. There was a slackness throughout the whole culture. But this time it's worse because it's not just financiers and speculators and bond traders, it's CEOs and CFOs ending up in handcuffs. That has not happened before.

We had the dot-com bubble which drove the NASDAQ up to 5,000, and now people have lost over 75 percent of their money.

No one looks at the rules anymore, not the SEC, not anybody. But when people begin to lose money, they get really mad. Then they get furious. They scream for blood, and that happens in every bubble.

I've made a study of these bubbles. The NASDAQ went from 1,200 to 5,000, now it's back to 1,200. At the top of the bubble, nobody gets excited about things that are, shall we say, "off color" or "shady," because everyone is making money. But when people become victims, the whole thing changes. And when the bubble is pricked and deflated, people get really mad.

I am mad about it. I'm real mad. I remember the movie *Network* with the line, "I'm madder than hell and I won't take it anymore."

That's how I felt today, seeing those guys taken out in handcuffs after they bought themselves condos and golf courses; I also applauded. It's a semblance of justice.

These offenders are going to have to go to jail with stiff sentences. That's what the public wants. When people saw handcuffs on the Rigases being taken off to jail—wow, we had a rally! That's what they needed. That's what they wanted, and it's usually that way at the end of a bubble.

People want blood. People want scapegoats. People have short memories; there will be another bubble, and the whole damn thing will begin all over again.

This is cyclical. If you study history you'll find that this is the story of almost any bubble. It's very hard to tell you're in a bubble while it's being created. Did you know this was a bubble while it was happening with the NASDAQ? Hardly anyone did. But now everybody knows it and that's when they need scapegoats and they want blood. Today is an emblematic day—the beginning of the reckoning.

We are not going to have the V-Shape recovery we had in 1987, which I would compare to a heart attack. This damn thing is more like a cancer. And while we can recover from cancer, it takes time. I think it will take a couple of years.

Notice we have a disconnect between the recovery, which seems to be pretty much on course, and the stock market, which ignores it. This is a problem because if the stock market collapses again, it might prevent the recovery from really moving on and we could have a double-dip recession.

You now have most of the American public profoundly involved in the stock market. This was not the case before. And they all are taking a beating. I know teachers who are virtually broke. I know doctors who have no retirement plan left because of this decline. This is serious.

I'm one of them. I have colleagues in the teaching profession and many friends in the professions whose retirement accounts are virtually wiped out. I'm lucky because I love what I do so I don't give a damn. I'll work 'til I drop because I love teaching and writing. But there are guys who looked forward to retirement who haven't got anything left. I feel for many of my friends who are absolutely wiped out.

People tend to panic at the bottom. Usually you reach the bottom when you see a panic. The Volatility Index reached an all-time high this morning, higher than the 9/11 period. It was up over 50, which is almost unheard of. Then I sensed we were close to the bottom. That's when they panic—what I call *get me out. Get me out at any price, I've had it, I can't take the pressure any more.* That's what you had this morning—July 24.

Typically, first rallies never hold. You have a rally which goes well, then they re-test the bottom again, scare the hell out of everyone one more time, and then it goes up. This process might take several months, and it's painful. I think you might see a slow recovery taking hold, but not the kind of recovery you had after the '87 crash.

The market troubles affect almost everybody and this never happened before. In '87 there were fewer people involved in the stock market than today.

People have always said if you buy and hold it will pay off. Well, baloney! Buy and hold is death. If you bought and held two years ago, you're dead. People don't know what to do now. Confusion reigns. This is now a trader's market, not a buy and hold market.

I'm a Holocaust survivor who escaped from Hitler, Stalin, Tojo, and Mao Tse-tung. I was lucky to survive and by all odds I should have been dead many times. But here I am, living near San Diego, teaching at a wonderful university, the University of San Diego, have great students, wonderful colleagues, and good friends, and Hitler is dead nearly sixty years, and I'm here. It's a Holocaust story with a good ending. There are not many of us around.

Despite the problems we have in the United States, when all is said and done, nowhere else in the entire world could I have built such a life and career as I've done in this country of freedom and opportunity. There is no country like this in the whole world.

Jim McIntyre

As senior deputy district attorney for Portland, Oregon, and head of the Violent Crimes Unit, McIntyre prosecutes people accused of violent crimes. He sees crime increasing and criminals becoming more violent. This trend began in the early 1980s, and he believes to a large extent it is a result of the breakdown of the family unit, with parents abdicating their authority and allowing their children to do as they please.

Every time I do a case, I look to see if it's sex, drugs, or money. Unfortunately, more often than not, it's drugs.

I have the most trouble with offenders in violent crimes using methamphetamine—like crack. Methamphetamine, being the cheap cocaine, is easily manufactured and easily obtained. It is highly addictive and [for] anyone who has a bent towards violence, it's going to take the edge off and let them be violent.

Heroin addicts, although they feel themselves invincible, are not usually out doing . . . they may do robberies and thefts to support their heroin habit . . . but when it comes to the slashings, the shootings, the road rage, parking lot rage, and domestic rage, if you're looking for a drug, it's going to be methamphetamine or cocaine based.

More than half of the people I try are on drugs, including alcohol. If you could take alcohol, methamphetamine, and cocaine out of the picture, you'd surely reduce violent crimes.

I see a lot more stealing to feed habits. I don't see many going to jail. The resources are limited so they're taking the petty offenders and shifting them into community courts and into diversion programs, keeping them out of the local jail facilities so there's more room for people who are doing violent crimes. People who are incarcerated for alcohol- and drug-related crimes make up nearly 95 percent of the prison population. This also includes those with mental deficiencies.

I go back and forth on the issue of interdiction and education. Some of the best programs in the country are directed at families to instruct their children as to how bad alcohol and narcotic substances are. We've gotten ourselves in a hell of a fix with my generation—the children of the '60s and the '70s—[by] taking such a soft stand on drug use. They have used it, their kids saw them using it, so the kids start using it, and the cycle continues.

The internal family education is extremely important. These ads about talking to your kids about marijuana, about alcohol—that's the best way to go.

At the other end of the spectrum, I don't have a problem with interdiction. When you look at the millions of dollars in the drug trade, interdiction with forfeiture laws and slamming assets is one of the most effective means we've got.

My generation, the people around me, the people I grew up with in high school and grade school, we are a funny generation. We were at the end of the free-love generation, and the '60s, but we weren't into the disco generation yet. There was a lot of marijuana, cocaine was around, and LSD was on the way out. That inbred an idea that *oh, it's not that big a deal.* Except the tide has turned. Marijuana growers are guarding their crops with automatic weapons.

Capitalism. Entrepreneurs. They make the weed more potent and charge more money for it. Start cornering the market. One of the down sides of interdiction is it's like stamping out cockroaches.

I used to live in row houses on the East Coast when I was in college. If you spray a row house for cockroaches, they move to the next row house. You shut down the marijuana coming across the Mexican border, and southern Oregon comes up with some of the best marijuana in the world.

Methamphetamine is a whole different ball game. I think methamphetamine has snuck up on the drug enforcement community because we were all focused outside the borders, focused on cocaine, heroin, and marijuana. Outlaw motorcycle gangs, Hell's Angels, those guys started to learn how to cook meth early and produce it in huge quantities out of these mobile laboratories, and it's turning out to be the internal cancer of the drug world.

For the most part, violent crimes don't happen to good people, to nice people. Violent criminals generally are from poverty, lower-income and lower-middle income groups, and their victims are from the same groups. It's not often you get a well-dressed businessman as a victim of even an armed robbery. But random street crime victims are at risk because they're out drunk at 2 A.M. or working the street as a prostitute or involved in a drug deal.

It's generally true that racial lines exist in crime. People tend to commit crimes within the community in which they live. So in my town, if you live in inner northeast and you're a criminal, you're going to probably do your crime in inner northeast, which means your victim's probably going to be African-American.

Criminals, number one, aren't very smart. Number two, they usually have addiction and mental problems. Number three, they don't have much need to travel. I did an aggravated murder case several years ago where two gang members killed a young girl for her car. Their idea of dumping her body in the woods was taking it to an inner city park and throwing it over the side of a cliff.

From their perspective, they took her to the country. Portland is a city where the river divides the middle and you count blocks east and west. Well, they dumped the body seventy-seven blocks east of the river. You can go 250 blocks before you begin hitting the countryside.

The late '80s is when things changed. When I started as a young prosecutor in 1981, the whole courthouse would stop for a murder trial. It was a big deal. You'd go down and watch, people would be talking about it for weeks and months on end. Now, we try murder cases around here and nobody even blinks an eye.

The average criminal just doesn't [care], which is scary. That is why we have 16-year-olds who are shooting people in the head and not thinking twice about it. Ten years ago that was not true. The bad guy is becoming more callous. It's part of the desensitization of these criminal acts. It doesn't affect them, why the hell do they care? I guess you're watching the offspring of the *me generation* taking *me* one step further.

Some of these guys are so institutionalized that prison is just going home. The outside is the strange part. These guys started in secure facilities when they were 14 years old. They don't commit crimes that will hold them for the rest of their life until they're about 25 to 30. It's nothing for them to go back.

You'll find they're coming from families where there's intellectual dysfunction, educational dysfunction, parents that never had much going to begin with. And then they get into drugs. They may be single-parent homes and the kids are basically left on their own to do whatever they want.

Or they're in homes where their parents are actually encouraging them or enabling them, never any sanctions imposed. The teachers are always wrong, the system's always wrong, the cops are always wrong, and the kid hears that over and over again so by age 14 well, hey, why not?

The biggest breakdown is in the family. If someone would have told me twenty years ago that I'd be saying this now I'd have told them they were out of their minds. There's not enough parental control, not enough education of parents on how to raise their children. People are having children and letting them do whatever the hell they want and we're all beginning to suffer the effects of it.

Up until the early '60s, parents raised and disciplined their children—taught them how to lead a proper life. Then in the '60s and '70s it was lead your life however you want. Everything's going to be fine. A big gap developed. Add narcotics and alcohol and, like I said, it's the *me generation* going one step further.

There is a segment of the Baby Boomers that has broken off into almost a subculture and they're just out of control. I'm almost a part of that generation and many of my friends are part of that generation and we have not broken off. We are prosecutors and lawyers and accountants and otherwise have survived that culture and are raising our kids, doing our best every day.

Doyle Hollister

Hollister is one of Southern California's most respected marriage and family therapists. With twenty-two years experience, he believes the main problem with married couples is their refusal to take responsibility for their own actions and blaming the other partner for the problems in the marriage. He sees depression becoming increasingly more prevalent, with men now developing eating disorders. On the plus side, he believes couples are more determined to stay together than in the past, thus helping to abate the disintegration of the American family.

Psychiatrists are medical doctors and people go to them for medicinal purposes and psychiatric disorders. Clinical psychologists, marriage family therapists, and social workers are specifically therapy oriented. It's not that psychiatrists don't do therapy, but at the very best they blend therapy with prescription medicine.

Back in 1975-76, when I went to school at Santa Clara, it was one of the few programs that specifically focused on marriage and family therapy. It was a new field then, a new degree. It wasn't so much focused on traditional analytic psychology, which is more long term, on-the-couch, individually based therapy. This was specifically focused on relationship therapy, marriages, families, etc.

At the heart of the family is marriage, and our culture is lacking significantly in how to make marriages work. We do not have much consciousness in terms of what a relationship even is and how it works in a functional way.

That's the dominant issue I deal with every day. I see marriage as the heart of the family and, of course, if the marriage doesn't work then the family doesn't stay together. Couples have a terrible time. Something like three out of five marriages end in divorce.

Oftentimes children are an identified symptom and underneath there is a relationship problem. Usually you can track back to some conflict that's being unaddressed, that's unresolved inside the marriage, and the children are brought into the middle of this and become symptomatic as a consequence.

That's one of the main theories behind family systems theory and I see that extensively in working with kids. Unless you work with the rest of the family, specifically with the issues in the marriage, you're not addressing the problem. You're just focusing on the symptom.

The main problem with couples is there is no real understanding of what it takes to have a functional relationship. What people need to do to make relationships work—there's a big blank there. The bottom line, the thing that I see every day, is a lack of personal responsibility, the willingness to deflect responsibility in terms of contributing to problems—blaming the other partner. This is what I struggle with every day—trying to get people to look at themselves in terms of their contribution to the problem rather than projecting blame onto the partner.

People don't want to look at their negative side, their dark side. They want to look at their partner's dark side and this is a huge problem. It goes beyond just marriage, it's an American cultural issue. Not taking personal responsibility for things we do that create certain responses in other people.

Americans are particularly reluctant to admit failure. People feel a sense of failure in their relationships all the time, but they don't want to verbalize and become vulnerable to that. They want to blame the failure on the other person. Failure is a real tough issue for us.

The issue of alcohol and drugs is rampant in families, and I look at it as symptomatic of something else. The dominant psychiatric disorder is depression. We have a depressive culture at this point. The question is, why is that? Why do we have so many people diagnosed with depression? Why do we have so many people on Prozac, Zoloft, etc., anti-depressants essentially?

There's something going on here. It's not that all of a sudden we just discovered that depression is an issue and we need to medicate. There's something culturally going on in terms of people being out of balance in some very specific way. Of the couples I see, one of the issues is the incredible stress they're trying to carry with dual career relationships, the struggle to make a buck in the United States to keep up with everyone else.

People are amazingly overloaded—it's a very fast-paced culture. People are getting progressively depleted and depressed, and that's a significant reason why marriages don't work. They have so little time, spend so little time, on the relationship. So much is spent on provider-ship, on just making a living, and the stress around that, putting in long hours of work. Two parents working, two different careers caus-es a lot of reverberation in terms of maintaining the relationship.

I have a daughter who is 15, and there's no question we wrestle as parents with the influence of image that comes at people relentlessly via MTV, *People Magazine*, fashion wear. The perfect image is such a focus—to conform to a perfect physical image and it's wreaking havoc on both male and female teenagers. Eating disorders with men is way up. It's becoming a real issue with young men, not just young women.

Much of my counseling is to help people manage on a more con-sistent basis problems they're going to be dealing with for the rest of their lives. Certain vulnerabilities, certain interactions, certain dynamics that they're going to struggle with forever, and the success is not to necessarily eliminate those problems, but to diminish the stress around them, diminish the threat to the relationship, and help people learn to manage, cope, and accept them.

Rather than *oh, we can never solve this, therefore let's split up,* if I can help people adapt to their inherent differences that cause conflicts, work with it, be less emotionally upset with it, I have made a major contribution to people's being able to stay together.

Again, the thing that is most frustrating is the difficulty I have with people accepting responsibility for their own faults, their own mis-takes, their contribution to why things don't work. Helping people to a consciousness of that and a comfort level of being able to own up to that. And then go from there, and the difficulty in trying to help people to not attack, not blame, just be honest and vulnerable, and go from there. To diminish their own destructive inputs and to take charge of their lives, their relationships, rather than expect the other person to make it work, that the other person is the problem.

Many people see me initially because they're surprised at who they married. The darker side of the person, which we all have, starts to emerge and they come in for early couples counseling. The next stage concerns early-age children because the transition for couples from no children to children is a very difficult transition and oftentimes couples start struggling because they don't know how to balance child care with marriage care.

That's a significant period. Another time zone is when people have reached a place of hopelessness and impossibility and come in as a last, desperate attempt to fix their marriage.

Unfortunately, that's a high percentage of what I get. But it's getting a little better in the sense that people are more conscious of trying to do something about their marriage earlier, trying to deal with issues before they become so emotionally hopeless and helpless. That's positive.

It's much more acceptable to see a counselor today than fifty years ago. You don't have to feel you're crazy. When I first started, the only people who would initiate therapy were women. There's more consciousness now, and men are more sensitive to the importance of relationships and they are initiating counseling more than they used to.

Another difficulty in marriage is we still in America don't have a solid sense of what is a male's and female's role in marriage. We're pretty screwed up there. We're still in a period of transition in terms of what is a man going to do, what is a woman going to do. It gets really complicated. I wrestle with many issues in terms of are we trying to change biology? That's complicated.

I see men and women more comfortable in being inquisitive about their relationship, [in trying] to get in and try to wrestle with this stuff. There's more of a willingness and a sense of need to do this. Over the last five years more people are trying to make marriages work. Before, I was experiencing people rejecting their marriages much more easily. Now I see a trend where people are trying to stay together.

Marriage is difficult, but it's the heart of the family, and our culture is struggling with the breakdown of the nuclear family, and the extended family. If I can work with these marriages and help people learn to maintain them and progress in them, I have done my job.

Tom Clarke

Clarke is a white 19-year-old student at Harvard who believes hip-hop and rap have no cultural value but are rather showmanship and production values. He believes it is the job of parents to keep things in perspective so that their children do not take the lyrics to heart and commit some stupid act. He does not believe popular music builds racial bridges. To him, a collateral benefit is that his parents hate it.

I am a sophomore at Harvard majoring in French and Francophone studies, which is mostly French literature, with some other disciplines. I have written several articles for the art section of *The Harvard Crimson,* which is the school daily newspaper. Music reviews comprise the bulk of my articles. I review a bunch of new CDs, generally rock, rap, and techno.

Music certainly changes. There's always a natural progression of styles and tastes, though the main themes under current popular music have remained the same. The popular artists are always the ones who combine a healthy sense of bravado with at least a bare minimum of musicianship to get by. The American public has never been too hard on its popular musicians. You can play three chords badly and still sell records.

As long as you have a strategy, you'll make it. Whether you play badly in earnest, whether you do it tongue in cheek, as long as you present yourself in a certain way and stick to it, it seems you'll find an audience in America, particularly among teenagers.

Hip-hop's been one of the major musical trends of my lifetime. As best I know, hip-hop was born in the late '70s when a guy in the South Bronx decided during the instrumental break in a reggae record that he would say some things over the instrumental part, and it just blossomed from there.

The reason hip-hop has taken off, at least among the white suburban kids who are buying the great majority of hip-hop records, is it's about bravado. And if that weren't true, then you see artists like Dead Prez and Common, who take a more political and intellectual approach to their music, selling just as well as Jay-Z, who talks about big pimping, spending cheese.

Lyrics have become more direct and to the point as our society has progressed, and you need to be more explicit and keep shocking people with the same regularity. Many viewed rock music or its various subcategories as a threat to Western Civilization. I think what may be changing is the ability of the audience to separate fact from fiction. In the past few years we've had countless examples of kids who just can't tell the difference between music expression, whatever you'd like to consider that as, and an actual suggestion.

A few years back, two kids were home alone and were playing a Snoop Dogg music video and one of the kids picked up a gun and was brandishing it saying, "I'm Snoop, I'm Snoop," making the same gestures he saw in the video. He ended up shooting his playmate.

It seems to me it's the character of the children, or the way they're being parented that is changing, not necessarily the relative danger of the music. The music I listen to contains any number of suggestions that would be illegal, deadly, immoral, or even worse if taken seriously. But I've never regarded it as anything more than a display of showmanship.

I don't think a white kid who listens to rap CDs would feel any more comfortable around a black person, certainly not in discussing the touchy subjects that need to be discussed before we can have racial reconciliation in our country, because the different audiences are buying into different things.

A white kid from the suburbs hears a rapper complain about the police and thinks, "Oh, yeah. I hate the police, too. They pulled me over for curfew violation and DUI at three in the morning when I was coming home from my friend's party." Whereas a black man buying that record may think, "I don't like the police because they stop me when they see me driving a nice car, thinking I might be a drug dealer."

There was a good article a few years ago in *Spin Magazine*. The title was something like "Why The White Boy Says 'Yo.'" The writer described the experience of going to a hip-hop concert and finding the audience was mostly suburban white kids. He asked some of the kids why they were there. Why they liked the music. Some kids said because we should all love the same music, racial conciliation, ya-da, ya-da, ya-da. One kid said, "I'm here because this music is about smoking weed and talking trash to cops."

I've never listened to music with the express intent of annoying my parents, but I wouldn't necessarily shy away from music to avoid annoying them either. Sometimes my mom will come upstairs and lean her head in the room and say, "That was a very charming line I just heard that young man shout," in reference to some horrible obscenity or slur that had just been used.

I hate to admit it, but what 18-year-old doesn't get a kick out of that? It's a benign form of rebellion in that I would never do any of those things, nor would I consider most of the other ways kids rebel against their parents.

Eminem is the only white hip-hop artist to really catch on. He makes money off the fact that he's a gleeful psychopath. And a funny one. And I like him for it.

Certainly hip-hop's influence is spreading. The big thing now is a fusion of heavy metal, rock, and rap styles, and in that genre it's perfectly okay for a white guy to be rapping. However, it's certainly not hip-hop in its traditional form.

In a musical sense, I regard guys like Chuck Berry and Fats Domino as ancestors of a sort. Their music certainly sounds dated today. It's not what you'd hear on a Top 40 station or at a party, but I realize that without that music nothing would be possible in the form in which I know it.

If Elvis Presley hadn't been shaking his hips and drawing criticism, and if we hadn't worked through that, we wouldn't have rappers being able to say what they say today. This goes back to every generation viewing rock music as a threat to civilization. Everything done in the past enabled the present to occur.

If you were able to meet your great-great-great-grandfather, you might not be able to relate to him in terms of popular culture, but you'd have a great deal of admiration and respect for him knowing he had made your existence possible.

Everybody my age would like to convince himself or herself that he or she will not sell out. Will not blindly stick to music that was only popular during their youth. We'd like to think we'll always be with the times, though I fear on some level its inevitable that I'll be flipping the radio dial one day and hear Eminem, and the DJ will make some sort of wisecrack, and I'll be slightly ashamed to admit I own that CD.

I'd love to convince myself that that won't happen, but I have a feeling it will. Everyone thinks they'll raise their children differently than they were raised, and then they have the epiphany they've become their parents.

Popular music provides the soundtrack to an adolescent's life. In my case, there's a whole class of songs which when I hear them I can identify with a particular age or particular experience. Not all the music-related memories from my adolescence are good.

In junior high, which is sort of a turbulent time for everyone whether they admit it or not, I listened to very angry music, and even though that's not as pleasant as a song I might be hearing now in college when things have become a little bit more stable, it's a very vivid memory.

When it comes to attaching memories to music, the most vivid come from adolescence. The song you heard when you first held a girl's hand will resonate with you and stick with you a lot more than the song you heard when you put together your first stock portfolio.

Allen Smith

Smith was at Pearl Harbor and served thirty-four years in the Navy, retiring in April 1970. People question whether today's youth are as effective as his generation. He is convinced that has nothing to do with the strength of American youth, but how strong and effective our technology is.

Until Pearl Harbor, in the so-called peacetime Navy, there was a definite hierarchy. If you didn't come from the Naval Academy, you really weren't in the "in" group, no matter what kind of an officer you were.

Enlisted men could be punished or put in the brig for almost anything—spitting over the side, spilling water. There was a real difference between the men and the officers. Once the war started, our freedoms increased.

When the war began, we became a team. This was very inspiring to me. Leadership was stronger and relationships had more meaning to them. It wasn't do this and do that, it was let's do this.

Blacks and Filipinos were in the Navy only as mess attendants and were totally segregated. By the end of the war it was obvious they were going to be brought on board and taken into the service. The NAACP came in to play and the black personnel were given different assignments. Harry Truman played a very important part in this. There was a lot of agitation by some people—the so-called redneck faction—who didn't go along with that. It was quite a thing to see.

The integration movement in America really began in the service.

It sure did. The billeting quarters, the quarters below deck, became integrated. We went to Cape Canaveral when I was in the manned spacecraft recovery system and the locals would not allow blacks in the motel with us.

Our chief of staff said, "We're going back to Norfolk." NASA really got after people—got after the town—and they rented condos and let all the blacks have a condo.

Today I see cells where you can't go safely. There are cells for the Vietnamese, the Hispanics. The blacks have come out into the neighborhoods and into the schools quite well. But others stay by themselves demanding things we didn't demand when we were growing up.

I come from a German background. I'm a Kraut and the Krauts were our enemies. It was a hard thing for me to endure during World War II because I was proud to be German. I thought Germans were real smart people. Now, people are coming over demanding their own language be used. Here in California, the voting forms are written in several languages, [as are] instructions for other things.

The country has progressed to the point where a gentleman my age can retire relatively safely with money in his pocket and can use the leisure time that has become available to him. This wasn't available to my father and he was disappointed, but was happy to have a television set in front of him when he got older.

Now we have so many great things, and not all [are] provided by government. They've been brought about by people like me. We've built our own senior centers. We're using the knowledge that we've gained as carpenters and wallpaper hangers and plumbers and electricians. We build our own buildings and we've just done wonderful things.

These things did not exist when I was growing up. My father was lucky to grow old with a family of young kids who were fairly prosperous and who could take care of him.

The values have changed so much. The value of adherence to good order and discipline has changed. We have moved from an agricultural nation to a manufacturing nation, to a country of business people.

Electronics was the big change. Radio changed the method of communication. It made things faster. We have all this stuff available to us, but it has made it more difficult to get to the truth. That bothers me. You have to read newspapers between the lines to figure out what some of these people are trying to say, what their real mission is. What is their real objective.

I love the old relationship between a boy and a girl. I thought that was wonderful. Now, all that has changed. It doesn't exist anymore.

If I were all of a sudden to be blessed with a 16-year-old girl that I had to be a father to, I would encourage her to get in there and dig. Go to college, do anything you have to—it's my responsibility to

teach you to take care of yourself. Mothers and fathers used to prepare their daughters for marriage so that they could take care of the
husband and the husband's mother.

I'm very optimistic about America's future. My only fear is the terrorists. We have put more effort in protecting our environment than
protecting ourselves against terrorists. There are people in the world
who want to kill us, who want to do us in.

We can no longer fight people man-for-man. We have to use our
technology. In his excellent book *Flags of Our Fathers*, James Bradley
explains [that in World War II the Japanese] would give hand
grenades to 18- and 19-year-old kids. The objective was to take the
grenade up the hill and toss it into a bunker. If he didn't make it, the
next kid took the grenade and went up. As many as five guys would
do that, just throwing men at it.

This changed when Norman Schwartzkoff said, "I don't give a
damn what Saddam Hussein does. I'm fighting my own war and he
better be ready for it." I hope we make a difference, make it so miserable for people to even plan to try and do anything bad to us.

We have to use our technology, so the whole meaning of the man
in the system has changed. You need the technology. You can have a
destruct system if you don't want the missile to continue on its
course. You can destroy it, you can alter it, you can change its course.
You can't recover it, of course, and that was one thing you could do
with a man.

The concept of putting the man in the system has really changed.
You've got to let these kids go with their computers and their imag-
ination. We can't fight people man-for-man anymore. We just can't
do it.

Jonathan Winters

In search of the Planet Ork.

I came to New York in January 1953, married with one child, with $56.46 to see if I could survive in the big time, and I did. It took a bit of doing, as it did for all of us at that time, or any time you go to New York or L.A. We all think we're prepared mentally, physically, and we've got enough money to last us, and we're fooled about every other day by what we've got in our wallets and in our minds.

Things that were happening then were the "Today Show" with Dave Garroway from Chicago. Jackie Gleason, Art Carney, and Audrey Meadows were going strong. That was a big evening on television to see them along with Sid Caesar and Imogene Coca. Of course, Milton Berle was king of comedy.

Arthur Godfrey had a tremendous following with the housewives, sitting with Tony Marvin and the rest of the gang commenting on Analoki and her ukelele, talking about Lipton Soup, and people would say, *Hey, wow, Godfrey's something else.*

Red Skelton at one time had an hour that belonged to him in the evening. I say *belonged to him.* He made a deal whereby he owned just that—one hour on CBS in the evening. That's not hearsay, because I took over Red's hour. We had to pay Red so much it was like renting. I never really understood it, but it gave me a season and a half with CBS and Red owned this hour. He and CBS. He [owned] all the shows he ever did on television and through his own choosing decided never to re-run them. So [the estate] is sitting on quite a bit of money.

I paint, write, and perform, and like to be able to censor my stuff before I'm told what I'm supposed to do on television or in the movies. What's happened, [people have] to drop their pants to get a laugh. Two of the funniest guys who ever lived—Laurel and Hardy—didn't drop their pants. They weren't dirty.

Halloween is all year round. They're all wearing an incredible amount of costumes. People are wearing furry shoes, pin-on mustaches, hair that sticks on the head, and many times go to bed in full make-up. A lot of people are putting a third eye in their forehead to draw attention to themselves at a football game. *Oh, look, pan in on this guy. This is wild. Look at this guy with the third eye.* A lot of people are auditioning.

I can remember a theater of 500 to 600 people seeing the movie *Gone With the Wind* when Gable turns to Vivien Leigh and she says, "Well what is to happen to me, Rhett? What am I going to do?" And he says, "Well, frankly, my dear, I don't give a damn."

Everybody went *Oh, geez.*

Well, we've gone from that to a lot worse.

What are you telling me? That's what I say to writers who are writing motion pictures and television. What are we offering up to our children? They're hearing this language at home, on television. Is this going to be their dialogue from now on? How does this help them? We're constantly seeing shows where everybody is a psychiatrist. Once a week people are telling the public how to react and what to do. This is very sad.

[Music today] has no lyrics that I can understand. I can understand Nat King Cole . . . *Unforgettable . . . ta, da, da, dee.*

What's going to happen as we look through this smog that envelops us in L.A.? It's not just in L.A. or New York, Chicago. . . . It's in Venice, Rome. It's causing the Appian Way to disintegrate, buildings in Venice.

People aren't eating fish as they used to. And if they do, they die of lead poisoning. Or, if they don't die of lead poisoning, then a truck overturns on the 101 and toxic poisoning kills all of Van Nuys.

We have to think to ourselves, *Are we going to survive or aren't we?* It doesn't mean that you have to become completely paranoid; I'm very close to that. So don't follow me all the way, but just think about it.

We have to consider going [further] out into space. We have the equipment, people, and the astronauts. The space program is one of the few programs I'm for.

I hope and pray there's a planet out there with all kinds of animals on it. I like to think there are rivers and lakes that are crystal clear and that when these guys in the silver suits and bubbles on their heads get off the space capsule and on to whatever planet it is, that they'll say, *Hey, you guys at NASA. The lakes are clear, several oceans here* and they're clear. We're able to see hundreds of feet down. Everything appears on the surface to be pretty good, but we haven't seen any life yet.

And then from out of nowhere comes a guy. Not a man with a hydrocephalic head, or with little carrot hands and five teeth and four eyes. He says, *Hey, how ya doing? You speak English? I sure do. Speak about twelve languages. You got to. Everybody reads up here. Don't come here smoking cigarettes, no booze, or drugs. We don't want to screw this one up. Please. We're from all over the universe. From different planets and if you don't like our way of life, then haul ass.*

Greg Clark

Clark was on the 62nd floor of World Trade Center Two on September 11, 2001. Incredibly, while he was in the process of exiting the building, someone announced over the public address system that everything was alright and that everyone should remain in their offices. Within a short period of time, the second plane crashed into the building. He credits the officers of the Port Authority with saving his life and the lives of many others in his building.

The plane hit World Trade Center One just as I reached the 62nd floor [of World Trade Center Two]. I was still in the elevator and the doors didn't open for a couple of minutes. I had no idea what happened, and was about to push the emergency button when they opened.

I walked out and took a few steps when nearly everyone on the floor ran around the corner very agitated. A couple of girls I work with said we had to get out, and they were really scared. I had no idea what was going on, but I turned around and the fire exit was right across the hall from the elevator and we began running down the stairs.

I then heard an American Airlines plane had hit Trade Center One, but I thought it was a little prop plane. At that point, people were cracking jokes, relatively relaxed going down the stairs. There was no panic, although my co-workers were scared, but things were pretty orderly and we were moving fast. I did sixty flights of stairs in less than ten minutes.

When we got to about the 10th floor, I heard someone announce on the loud speaker: *"All World Trade Center employees in Two World Trade Center, there's been a fire in World Trade Center One. It's contained. Everybody please stay in your offices."*

I'm still in the stairwell. I had gone down fifty flights of stairs and I wanted to finish the job, so I kept running. There were people who had been there in '93 and they weren't about to stop. One of the women I was with had children and she wanted to get out—she had been there in '93. It was still pretty orderly.

I opened the door. It was a perfect sunny day. I was looking south toward the Statue of Liberty out in the harbor. Across the street was a parking lot and I noticed cars were on fire, debris everywhere, everything was covered in ashes. I remember a ring of people staring at us. It was crazy, it looked like a war scene, but the second plane had not hit yet.

I thought I better get out of there. Time [sequence] is hard to remember that day. I've been able to put it together by reviewing news reports when different events happened.

I had to walk around to the stairwell that went down to the basement level, but I found myself staring out the windows at what was going on. Then I started walking. In between the two towers was a big plaza with a fountain in the middle and that was covered with seats and pieces of the airplane. Things were on fire. That's when I noticed a person hit the ground.

I thought, *Oh, my God, that was a person.* The body resembled tomatoes. It was just splat, and I just . . . oh Jesus. I was right in the middle of all this stuff coming down, the most dangerous place to be. There was stuff falling all over the place.

I walked toward the Church Street side of the building, which is the eastern side of the two towers. I was trying to get to that side 'cause I figured that would be the safest way to get out. We were jogging and it was relatively orderly. Then someone said it was closed, you couldn't get out that way. People didn't know where to run.

We were going back when the second plane hit. *BOOM,* there was this huge shaking, and it reminded me of a school of minnows when you throw something at them and they explode in every direction. Chaos. Everything was shaking, like an earthquake, people going nuts, panicked. I was panicked. I ran underneath a storefront because you hear when an earthquake hits to go underneath a door so if the building's going to collapse you have the structure to protect you.

I saw the girls I was with a little ways away and ran over to them and said, "Let's get out of here." So we went into the subway and all the way down the platform to the other end, which got us out about a block north of the Trade Center complex, the Chamber Street exit.

Now people were panicked and it was a jammed spot, so getting out of there was hectic. We had no idea an airplane had hit our building. It was scary 'cause we thought it was going to come down on us, that somebody was trying to kill us. We looked up and saw both buildings on fire, people jumping. This is something you push from your mind.

We ran across town toward City Hall and saw people running in the other direction—toward the buildings. I hope that they changed their minds 'cause the building would have come down on top of them. We got to City Hall and decided to start going uptown.

That's when the buildings must have been getting weaker because police were saying over loudspeakers, "Go uptown, everybody uptown."

It was like those monster movies where you have thousands of people running through the streets getting away from something. It was something I never thought I would experience. There's nothing like it.

My first reaction was get the bleep out of Manhattan, but you couldn't. We all went to a friend's apartment and then I met my roommate, and I had to find my girlfriend, who worked near the New York Stock Exchange. I was afraid she ran toward the buildings, and then I heard that the buildings had collapsed.

At the end of the day, things started sinking in. My whole department, everybody that I knew from Morgan Stanley, was on the 74th floor. I had been moved to the 62nd floor a few months earlier. I had no idea what happened to them . . . if they had survived. I broke down pretty badly. Not knowing if all these people were alive or dead. That was the worst part of the day.

I no longer feel as secure as I once did. No way you can after you have something like that happen. Why does this have to happen? Why can't we defend ourselves against something like that?

It makes me more aware of life. That day things broke down very quickly to literally life and death emotions and what's really important in life. Your family number one, friends, shelter, security.

The Port Authority were the ones that saved my life. There was a lot of chaos and they were organized and got us to safe exits. They stayed there until the end, until it came down on them.

David McCullough

Pulitzer Prize winning historian McCullough believes that September 11, 2001, was the worst day in American history, but that the early days of World War II were darker. He believes that September 11 has awakened the country, that courage is back in fashion, patriotism is embraced, that we are the United States of America and no one is going to take our way of life away from us. Amen.

September 11, 2001, was the worst day in American history. Having said that, I also believe we have been through worse times, more difficult times, darker times than we are living in now in the months since September 11. What was so terrible about September 11 was not just the magnitude of the massacre but the fact that it came out of the blue, literally and figuratively, without any warning, in peacetime, on our own home ground.

Pearl Harbor was far, far away and most Americans didn't even know where it was. The world was at war. We weren't, but it was apparent we were going to be at war. Pearl Harbor was a military attack, on a military target, and the loss of life was less. It was a horrible day, and in many ways its importance in retrospect is clearer than the importance of September 11 because we know where it fits in in the large story, the large, tragic, hideous story of World War II.

We don't know yet how long the present crisis will last. We don't know if it's going to get worse. We don't know what ultimately the costs are going to be. But as an outright vicious murder, as a terrifying spectacle on television, there is nothing in our experience to match it. You'd have to go back to the Civil War to find such bloodshed on our own home ground as took place in New York, Washington, and Pennsylvania.

I expect September 11 will be seen in retrospect as the time we recognized globalization wasn't just a theory, it was a fact of life. That it isn't just a mercantile or financial idea, one that includes great opportunities and great benefits, but also great dangers and evil. That we better wake up to securing our safety as a nation, our means of protection.

We must realize we have no choice. Like it or not, we're now part of a world which has been dealing with terrorism for quite some time. It is no longer just happening in Ireland or England or Israel or some Middle Eastern country. It's here and we're part of it now, like it or not.

The selfishness, self-indulgence, self-aggrandizement, hedonistic romp we were on is over. It already looks not only far in the past, but passé, and immature and no longer relevant. The painful wounds of September 11 are going to be felt for as long as we live, and the healing process is going to be longer than we expect.

There's much to be proud of about the country now. The mayor of our greatest city and our president rose to the occasion as well as any public servants have at any time. We've seen real heroism, not celluloid or contrived heroism, take place before our eyes. That so many of those firefighters and police and those men on the plane that went down in Pennsylvania were all young people is not to be ignored.

This is the generation that many of us were saying, and I'm at fault, too, were adrift without objectives, were spoiled, soft. They, by all means, are not. They've shown us what courage is. Courage is back in fashion. Patriotism is not thought to be corny now or a sign of little education or sophistication. We're united in a way that we haven't been almost in memory. And we are determined to do what has to be done.

There's no question that we will come through. We will prevail. We will be stronger for it. We'll go forward. The awful experience of September 11 has made us take stock of what really matters in our lives, what we really value, what we really will fight to hold on to. It's been a healthy exercise in taking inventory of our values.

We are a nation of surpassing strength, the most productive nation in the world. We are the most ingenious, the most inventive, the most creative, and the most generous nation in the world. And our natural resources are extraordinary. Again, surpassing. But we must never forget that our most valuable of all resources is our brainpower. Our capacity to use our minds and to keep our heads.

We have a further source of strength which fortunately is inexhaustible, and that's our story, our history, our record as a people. We have only to draw on that, not just for inspiration but for a sense of who we are and what we can do. We have come through dark times in the past, back to before the Revolution, through the Revolution, the Civil War, World War I, the terrible horrors of the influenza epidemic, the Depression, World War II—there's never anything inevitable about history.

Nothing has ever had to happen, the way it happened. There was no guarantee that we would crush the Nazi machine. The last months of 1941, the first months of 1942, were about as dark a time as there ever was for civilization. The Germans were using their submarines to sink our oil tankers off the coast of Florida and New Jersey, right within sight of shore.

There was nothing we could do about it. We had an Army that was pathetic by world standards. Our recruits were drilling with wooden rifles. We had virtually no Air Force. Half of our Navy had been destroyed at Pearl Harbor. The German army was at Moscow, they controlled North Africa. England was on its last legs. It was a very bleak time.

Churchill came across the Atlantic and made a very important speech in late December 1941. He said, "We haven't journeyed this far because we're made of sugar candy." That's really what we need to remember. Who do these people think they are, that they can imagine terrifying us to the point of immobility. Terrifying us with their cowardly acts of murder into a position where we will do their bidding. We will rise to the occasion. We will do what has to be done, and let's hope that it can be done quickly. I have no doubts whatsoever that we will prevail and be stronger for it.

You fly across this great country as I have and you look down and see how large it is, and how green, and the farms and the roads and the bridges and the cities—all that we've built. All that those before us have done on our behalf. Our freedoms. Our opportunities. Our system of education. Are we going to let anybody take that away from us? Absolutely not!

Epilogue

David McCullough remarked how impressed he is every time he flies across America and observes the monuments to progress we have built, which in turn will be passed on to other Americans: cities, highways, bridges, waterways, and homes all underlining our accomplishments, testimony that Americans would fight to the last to preserve their way of life.

America has made great strides forward the last fifty years. This was accomplished despite wars in Korea and Vietnam, turmoil resulting from the civil rights struggle, serious cultural conflicts, enormous time and resources devoted to winning the Cold War, and political leadership that for the most part was lacking; in the cases of Johnson, Nixon and Clinton, it was destructive.

The nation began the second half of the 20th century absorbed with Joseph McCarthy and the war in Korea. Communism was on everyone's lips and until Edward R. Murrow's television program on March 9, 1954, denouncing McCarthy, followed by the Army-McCarthy Hearings the next month which finished McCarthy as a political force, we had become a country devouring ourselves.

The 1950s have been belittled as a do-nothing decade, but Ike kept us out of war, built the interstate highway system, and the country was prosperous. Network television went coast-to-coast, and Dick Clark was the man, with Rock 'n' Roll annoying everyone over the age of 24. Movies that drew over 50 million weekly during the war were hurting. Louis Mayer was out, Jack Warner was scrambling, Harry Cohn was dead, and Darryl Zanuck was riding into the sunset; no one had a solution for how to defeat television and regain past glory.

John Kennedy wished to expand our presence in the world, but Russia was still the Bear. He pushed for civil rights as far as the political climate permitted. His assassination changed the tone of the country and we became more cynical.

Lyndon Johnson upped the ante in Vietnam, at the same time knowing we could not win the war. He tried to "out-New Deal" Roosevelt with his Great Society, but it proved unsuccessful. He alienated the young people with Vietnam and white people with the Great Society because it did not benefit them. Johnson trounced Goldwater in 1964, but two years later the Republicans began their move in the off-year elections, gaining the White House in 1968 with Nixon's election.

By 1969 even the pro-war people realized the light at the end of the tunnel was an illusion. Student and street demonstrations were becoming more violent. A year earlier, the turbulent Democratic Convention in Chicago had cost Hubert Humphrey the election.

Older Americans began to believe they were losing the country that only twenty-five years earlier they had fought to defend. They could not comprehend the everyday violence and language, Elvis was barely digestible, and who dressed the Jefferson Airplane and Grand Funk Railroad? It was about time the Smothers Brothers were dropped by CBS. And have you seen this new show with this guy named Archie Bunker?

Just when people thought it could not get any worse, we learned of the Cambodia invasion, followed by Kent State. After Nixon crushed McGovern, Watergate was exposed, resulting in Nixon's resignation in 1974. Ford pardoned Nixon, assuring Carter's election in 1978.

The '70s were coming to an end with its war, protesters, drugs, hard rock, vulgarity, and Nixon's resignation. Oil shortages, stagflation, the attacks on established institutions—it was a decade to remember, and to forget.

It was hard not to like Ronald Reagan. He reminded Americans of what we stood for and the great things that were still ahead of us. After twenty years of national torment, he was just what the doctor ordered. Much brighter than given credit for, he realized Russia was nearing the end economically and informed Gorbachev that we were going forward with Star Wars, that he was increasing our military budget, and that he backed the other side in Afghanistan.

After a forty-four-year Cold War, communism began breaking apart in the Baltic States and Poland, spreading to the other satellites. The Wall came down in Berlin. Gorbachev tried to make concessions, but it was too late. Russia imploded. Marx was wrong.

The Gulf War revealed the high level at which our military now operated. People rushed home from work to witness our latest military feat on television; the Gulf War lasted about as long as Pauly Shore's movie career.

The war's success though was not enough to overcome George Bush's "Read my lips, no new taxes" gaffe. Clinton defeated him in 1992 and spent the next eight years administering a good economy and running focus groups to determine the proper buzz words to use—"I feel your pain" and "your children" being two of his most successful.

Clinton knew that his generation—the Baby Boomers—identified with him. They represented 60 percent of the country, and though they might not agree with his actions, they were inclined to give him a pass. He was very astute politically—possibly the most adept American politician of the 20th century—but few wished to emulate him.

He was a cultural disaster, and the thoughtful among us realized that his malpractice with the truth, his spectacular self-centered behavior, and his aversion to honesty represented the worst of the preceding thirty-five years.

Pearl Harbor shook us from the dream of isolation; September 11, 2001, shook us from our complacency. As with Pearl Harbor, we were shocked and disgusted. Then, with measured anger, we attacked the enemy.

President Bush did not pose next to the problem, nor overpromise and underdeliver. He acted promptly and effectively. Our military, composed of a new generation of fighting men and women, performed magnificently.

Americans walk straighter now. They no longer feel uncomfortable to talk patriotically, to fly the flag, to cry when they hear "God Bless America," and to sing our National Anthem with deep feeling.

It is good to be home again.

Index